Mira Silverstein's
GUIDE TO
SLANTED STITCHES

Books by Mira Silverstein include:

FUN WITH BARGELLO

FUN WITH APPLIQUÉ

BARGELLO PLUS

INTERNATIONAL NEEDLEWORK DESIGNS

MIRA SILVERSTEIN'S GUIDE TO UPRIGHT STITCHES

MIRA SILVERSTEIN'S GUIDE TO LOOPED AND KNOTTED STITCHES

MIRA SILVERSTEIN'S GUIDE TO SLANTED STITCHES

MIRA SILVERSTEIN'S GUIDE TO COMBINATION STITCHES

Mira Silverstein's

GUIDE TO SLANTED STITCHES

xxxxxxxxxxxxxxxxxxxxxxxxxxxxxxxxxxxxxxxxxxxxxxxxxxxx

Exciting Needlework Projects, Patterns, and Designs Anyone Can Make

ARTWORK BY ROBERTA FRAUWIRTH

PHOTOGRAPHS BY SANDY L. STUDIOS

DAVID McKAY COMPANY, INC.
New York

I wish to take this opportunity to thank all those who worked with me in a professional capacity and especially Barbara Anderson who helped edit this book.

Samples finished by Ida Gold, Harriet Alonso, Carol B. Kempner, Mindi Kantor, Shirley Kantor, Elise Silverstein, Gigi Strauss, Joan Hyman, Mary McGregor, Eve Charny, Marie Gunther, and Jane Benson.

Diagrams on pages 90, 124, and 125 by Shirley Rose.

For Josh

Library of Congress Cataloging in Publication Data

Silverstein, Mira.
 Mira Silverstein's Guide to slanted stitches.

 1. Canvas embroidery.   I. Title.   II. Title: Guide to slanted stitches.
TT778.C3S543   1977   746.4'4   77-10839
ISBN 0-679-50819-8
ISBN 0-679-50783-3 pbk.

10 9 8 7 6 5 4 3 2 1

Manufactured in the United States of America

Designed by Jacques Chazaud

CONTENTS

INTRODUCTION   7

IMPORTANT INFORMATION FOR THE BEGINNER   9
   Threading the Needle and Anchoring Yarn   9
   How to Read and Interpret Diagrams and
     Graph Outlines   10
   How to Enlarge and Transfer Designs   11
   Fabric   13
   Mending Torn Canvas   17
   Yarns   18
   Tools   19

SLANTED STITCHES   20
   Half-Cross Stitch   20
   Tent (Continental) Stitch   22
   Basketweave (Diagonal Tent) Stitch   25
   Slanting (Oblique) Gobelin Stitch   29
   Encroaching Gobelin   31
   Kelim (Kalem) Stitch   33
   Slanted Stitch Patterns   36
   Mosaic Stitch Pattern   37
   Scottish (Scotch) Stitch Pattern   39
   Cushion Stitch Pattern   39
   Cashmere Stitch Pattern   44
   Checks (Chequer) Stitch Pattern   46
   Milanese Stitch Pattern   48
   Byzantine Stitch Pattern   50
   Jacquard Stitch Pattern   53
   Running Stitch, Back Stitch, and Stem Stitch 54
   Cross Stitch Patterns and Textures   55

Fern Stitch Pattern 61
Web Stitch Pattern 63
Knotted Stitch Pattern 65
Herringbone Stitch 67
Four-way Herringbone Stitch Pattern 71
Norwich (Waffle) Stitch Pattern 74

PROJECTS 79
Distortion in Slanted Stitches 79
Cut-away or Waste Canvas 84
Tricycle Seat Cover 88
Alphabet 91
Tumbling Blocks 93
Small Interwoven Patterns 96
Houndstooth Pattern 97
Gingham 98
Woven Ribbons 99
Borders and Small Patterns 100
Purses 103
Lacy Window Hanging 104
Beaver 107
Tennis Racquet Cover with Sneakers 108
Doll Pillow 109
Bokara Design 110
Two-color Floral Design 111
Eagle 112
Leopards 113
Poppies 116
Background Stitches: Flat, Trellis, and Shaded 117

FINISHING AND MOUNTING NEEDLEWORK 120
Blocking Needlework 120
Framing Needlework 123
Mitering Fabric 126
Making a Needlepoint Pillow 126

LIST OF SUPPLIERS 127

XXX

INTRODUCTION

Needlework is the general term used to describe all work done with the threaded needle, both by hand and by machine. It is divided into two main categories: utilitarian needlework or sewing, where stitches perform the basic function of joining fabrics; and decorative needlework, where stitches are used to create a design which decorates the fabric surface and becomes part of the fabric itself.

There are various kinds of decorative needlework. The most familiar are listed below.

Embroidery is a term most often used to describe decorative needlework applied to fine, densely woven fabrics, such as linen, silk, or cotton.

Crewel is embroidery worked with wool yarn or yarns of similar texture on compatible fabrics, such as linen or wool.

Canvas work refers to the kind of fabric used and not a special kind of needlework. Canvas is an open-mesh, even-weave fabric and the stitches worked on it will be a little more "patterned," or uniform, than those worked on denser cloth.

Counted-thread indicates the manner of workmanship when the design is not painted on the fabric but is reproduced from a graphed outline. The graph is counted in stitches or stitch units, and the fabric is counted in threads. The more threads alloted to a stitch unit, the larger the gauge of the design.

Surface embroidery is a figure of speech since all embroidery is worked on the surface.

Needlepoint is sometimes used to describe canvas work in general and the Half-cross or Continental Stitch in particular. However, it is not a stitch. It is only another term for work with a threaded needle, or "point of the needle."

Creative stitchery refers to the most artistic form of needlework when the stitches are used to create an original design on the fabric rather than first painting the design on the fabric and then filling it in with stitches. Creative stitchery is also a general term for embroidery or stitchery. It is the art or craft of decorating fabric with lines and loops in interesting patterns with the aid of a threaded needle. The lines and loops are known as stitches.

The basic, or line, stitch is a straight line between two points and is executed with a threaded needle. The threaded needle is brought to the surface of the fabric, carried across it in a predetermined direction, then brought back to the reverse side of the fabric to complete the stitch.

The line stitch may be long or short, horizontal or vertical, or slanted to any degree; but in itself it is only a line. Worked end to end, the line stitch will, in some cases, form a curvilinear outline. However, it cannot curve or flex by itself without being anchored in some way by another stitch, in which case the line stitch is altered before completion. All knotted, looped, chained, and tied stitches are based on this manipulation.

When a number of line stitches are worked side by side, crossed over, or placed in any combination to form a specific pattern, they create what is called a stitch formation, or stitch pattern.

Each stitch formation has its own distinctive texture when worked over a large area. This texture is immediately altered with the slightest adjustment in the length and number of lines in the individual stitch pattern.

There are hundreds of stitch patterns in the lexicon of needlework. They are often identified by name and place of origin. Most of them are minor variations of a handful of classic patterns.

This is a beginners' introduction to basic decorative needlework. The accent is on the construction of stitches and stitch patterns that, once mastered, will enable the beginner to create a wide variety of beautiful and useful projects. Each stitch and stitch pattern will be outlined in step-by-step detail, and its special properties and usage will be explained. Many design projects are introduced in this book. However, beginners are encouraged to further diversify and explore, to invent new stitch patterns, to create unusual color combinations, and to alter, adapt, or adjust. The possibilities are endless.

XXX

IMPORTANT INFORMATION FOR THE BEGINNER

Threading the Needle and Anchoring Yarn

For those who have never worked with canvas and yarn, a little practice is recommended before embarking on a large project. The best way to learn anything is by doing.

Read the sections on materials and supplies and buy a small piece of firm, interlocked # 12 canvas, a few small skeins of Persian-type yarn in assorted colors, and a blunt-pointed needle.

Cut the canvas into small easy-to-handle pieces, and cover the edges with paper or plastic tape. (Surgical and cellophane tapes will not adhere properly to canvas.) Even if the canvas does not ravel, the edges are rough and should be taped.

To thread the needle, fold the end of a strand of yarn over the needle and hold both firmly between thumb and forefinger. Pull the needle away without disturbing the yarn fold. Press the fold between the fingers until yarn is flat and barely visible. Press the eye of the tapestry needle over this fold and don't release the yarn until the needle is threaded.

To begin work on a bare canvas, pull the threaded needle up through the fabric, leaving a tail of about 2" on the reverse side. Hold this tail down with one hand while you work the first few stitches over it, catching some of the yarn in the process.

Subsequent strands should be slipped through a worked area and held in place for the first stitch or two. Don't use knots in canvas work—they can almost always be detected. If a knot becomes undone, there probably won't be enough yarn to reanchor it, and several stitches may have to be taken out and replaced.

To end off the yarn, slide it into a worked area and keep all visible tails clipped. Tails will tangle the working yarn and the wool will shed a fuzz which will carry onto the right side of the work and become imbedded in the stitches.

How to Read and Interpret Diagrams and Graph Outlines

The designs in this book are shown in diagrams or graph outlines. A *diagram* is the outline or framework of a needlepoint design. A diagram is shown complete on one page or in sections on two or more pages. Yarn colors are outlined within the diagram and indicated by numbers.

To transfer a diagram to canvas, you must first reproduce it on another sheet of paper as is, or enlarge it if necessary. The canvas is then placed over this paper and the design traced with a fine-point, indelible pen.

Any diagram can be altered and the stitches changed to suit the individual needleworker. Parts and pieces from one diagram may be combined with those of another to create any number of design variations.

A *graph* is a skeletal construction of a design. It shows not only the design outline but each and every stitch within it. The colors are indicated by such symbols as half-crosses, crosses, lines, dots, etc. The code is shown in the corner of the page.

A graph is also called a counted-stitch pattern because it is reproduced stitch for stitch and not within a drawn outline. This is the most accurate way to reproduce a needlepoint design, but it allows little room for creative alterations.

The graphs shown in this book should be worked in cross or half-cross stitches.

To reproduce a counted-stitch pattern, divide the canvas into a number of equal squares. Draw the lines over the canvas threads with fine-point acrylic pen. Although the stitches are painted inside the graph squares, they are worked *over* the canvas threads or meshes, and this is the way they should be translated.

Graph paper is generally divided into small squares of ten or more to the inch. The square inch is outlined with a heavier line,

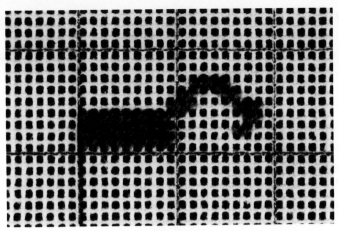

FIGURE 1

Creating a grid to facilitate counted thread stitchery

which makes the counting of stitches much simpler.

By turning your canvas into a graph (Figure 1), the stitch-by-stitch count becomes less formidable.

Begin at any point, and work the groups of stitches in consecutive order. Do not skip from one area to another. Complete the entire design before doing the background. If a graph design seems too complicated, color in the coded stitch outlines. Use transparent colors that are bright enough to show color placement without covering the code marks. To enlarge a graph pattern, use a canvas with a larger gauge.

Note: Graph outlines should be drawn on canvas that will be covered completely with stitches. If the background is to be left unworked, mark the dividing lines in soft pencil that can be erased where needed. Pre-test all pens and pencils.

When a design outline is shown in counted stitches, it may be reproduced stitch-by-stitch or placed under the canvas (enlarged if necessary) and outlined in the same manner as a diagram. The geometric lines seem to round out and soften when viewed under a canvas mesh.

How to Enlarge and Transfer Designs

To transpose a design onto needlepoint canvas, the design must first be transferred to a flat sheet of paper. If the design is shown in actual size, make a photocopy of the page. If the design is shown in sections, photocopy all the sections and assemble them into one design. Tape the design copy to a flat surface, and place the canvas over it. If the lines are not clearly visible, go over them with a black marking pen.

Position the canvas over the paper to center the design, and place a few push pins all around to prevent it from shifting. Allow a proper margin all around: 2" for soft pillows, handbags, and wall hangings; and 3" or more for work to be framed or upholstered. Trace the design outline with a fine-point acrylic pen, outlining shapes, colors, features, etc.

Color in the canvas, using the suggested color key or your personal preference. If you have some artistic ability and would like to create your own design, keep it simple at first. Never place a design directly on canvas without first working it out on paper. Bear in mind that the more complicated the design outlines, the finer the canvas and the smaller the stitches should be.

Any paint can be used as long as it is smudge-proof—by this, I mean any paint, pencils, or colored pens that do not rub off on your hand as you work. No media is completely waterproof, except oil and acrylic paints. Both require a certain amount of artistic training to use properly, and the acrylics will often flake off a heavily sized canvas. Any needlepoint canvas that was painted in oils should never be sent to professional dry cleaners. The solvents used in such cleaning establishments may loosen the oils and bring them to the surface—with disastrous results.

For best results, use acrylic pens or light-colored felt markers. They needn't match the yarns exactly. There is no need to wet needlepoint, as you will see in the instructions for blocking, and professional cleaning will eliminate felt markings without a trace. Pre-test all paints on a scrap of canvas before applying them to actual canvas.

When the design outline is shown reduced in size, the actual dimensions are indicated on the same page. The easiest and most accurate enlarging method is photostating. Check with local newspapers or printing shops for the photostat service nearest you. A photostat is *not* the same as a photocopy. Photocopy machines, available in most libraries and general stores, will duplicate a sheet of paper no larger than legal size. Photostat machines, on the other hand, can enlarge or reduce a design to any size desired. Before enlarging, check the design carefully for any changes you may wish to make. Obliterate unwanted portions with white poster paint, and draw any additions with a black felt-tip marking pen.

The alternative to making a photostat is the square-by-square method of enlarging. Draw a margin all around the design (if there isn't one already) and divide the area into sixteen equal squares or rectangles. Do this by measuring and dividing the pattern in half and then in quarters, both vertically and horizontally. Take a sheet of paper the size of the desired enlargement, outline the margin, and divide it into the same number of squares or rectangles as the original pattern. For a complicated design, subdivide the squares into thirty-two smaller ones. Number the squares in sequence on both the design and the proposed enlargement paper, and then copy the design square-for-square. The accuracy of the enlargement will depend on individual artistic ability. Remember to make all necessary alterations at this time.

A design may be reduced in size in the same manner that it is enlarged. Make all changes *after* the reduction is completed.

Note: The canvas gauge is indicated in each design outline. You may use a smaller-gauge canvas if you wish to work with finer stitches. Do not use a larger mesh canvas unless you enlarge the design proportionately. For example, if a design is shown on # 10 canvas and you wish to work it in # 5 mesh, enlarge the design to double the size indicated in the instruction guide.

Fabric

Needlepoint canvas is the most familiar of the background fabrics. It is an even-weave cotton fabric with open meshes that are easy to count. There are two basic types of canvas: single-thread, or mono; and double thread, or Penelope.

Mono canvas is a simple weave of single vertical and horizontal threads. (Figure 2, A and D.) It comes in stark white as well as a variety of colors and its smooth, flat surface is ideal for tracing and painting designs. Mono canvas is best suited for the Straight

FIGURE 2
A, # 12 Mono canvas (interwoven) in tan; B, # 5 Double thread canvas in white (suitable for rugs); C, # 12 Mono canvas (interlocked); D, # 10 Mono canvas (interwoven) with raveled threads. Finished edges are called selvedge.

Gobelin or Bargello needlework. It is a standard, loosely interwoven fabric with durable threads that can withstand a great deal of wear and tear. It is recommended for large projects, especially those that will be used in upholstery.

There is a new interlocked mono canvas (Figure 2, C) which features smooth, flat threads that do not unravel easily. It is an excellent choice for small projects. The interlocked canvas is not recommended for needlework that requires extensive blocking because the lightweight threads tend to break when stretched.

Double-thread, or Penelope, canvas is the most durable of the needlepoint canvases. (Figure 2, B.) It is excellent for rugs or chairseat covers. In most cases it will outlast the yarn after many years of wear. It is much easier to repair a worn piece of needlework by replacing stitches on a still-durable canvas than it is to insert patches of fresh canvas into a deteriorating background.

The double threads may be pushed apart with a needle and worked in finer stitches or petit point. This is especially useful when working a design that has some areas of fine detail, such as facial features, hands, etc.

Penelope canvas is available in gauges up to # 3½, which is sometimes known as quick-point canvas.

A canvas of good quality is firm but not rigid. The mesh threads run straight and true, and the knots that re-tie broken threads are far apart and barely visible.

Freshly unrolled canvas may seem a little crooked, but a good tug at opposite corners should straighten it out. A very firm canvas that resists the tug may be relaxed by giving it a light steaming and then pulling it back into shape before it dries and regains its firmness.

Needlepoint canvas is always coated with a special starch called sizing. This gives it body and a firm support for stitches. An open-mesh cotton fabric would otherwise be limp, and the mesh threads would lose their form under the pressure of the heavy yarns. The stitches would look uneven and the over-all effect would be unattractive.

Starched, or sized, fabric is essential for all work that will require blocking. In the blocking process, a distorted canvas is pulled back into shape and nailed to a board. The sizing is softened by steaming. As it dries, it regains its firmness as well as its original shape. (For more information, see the section on blocking.)

Canvas is sold by gauge number. The gauge is the number of meshes, or threads, within a linear inch. The greater the number of threads, the finer the canvas holes. Ask for canvas by number and type of weave: # 10 mono canvas is a single-thread canvas with ten meshes to the inch.

Canvas is available in a wide selection of colors in addition to the traditional white and tan. A novelty color is desirable only when large portions of the canvas fabric are to be left unworked. Otherwise, use white for needlework with light colored yarns and tan for projects with darker yarns.

Stark white canvas will sometimes show through black or very dark backgrounds. If tan canvas is not available, tint the white canvas with tea or coffee. Pour a medium-strength solution of cooled tea or coffee into a basin. Dip the canvas for a few minutes, and then dry it on a flat surface. If the canvas is wrinkled, press it with a hot iron over a damp cloth. The stain will be a uniform tan color. Be sure to cool the liquid before dipping your canvas. If the liquid is hot, it will wash away the sizing, leaving your canvas limp.

If the canvas does become limp, however, you can renew its freshness with some spray starch and a light ironing. If the canvas becomes limp while you are working on it, steam press on the reverse side and let it dry. If this does not seem to help, cover the reverse side with a light cotton cloth, spray it with starch, and press over it. Let it dry before resuming work.

Rya cloth (Figure 3, A) is a specially woven fabric for Rya or Turkish knots. Open mesh and closely woven rows alternate to create even spacing between the rows of loops. Rya is a durable fabric and makes an excellent background for the heaviest looped rugs as well as multiple Herringbone stitchery. It comes in 36" width and in gray only.

FIGURE 3
A, Rya cloth;   B, Demo double mesh light-weight novelty cloth.

Demo (Figure 3, B) is a wide, open double-mesh cloth. It is not as durable as standard Penelope rug canvas, nor is it as heavily sized, but it does provide a beautiful backing for heavy craft yarns worked in large textured stitches. Demo does not need complete coverage. Demo is available in colors.

The above fabrics may be purchased at most needlework shops, or see the List of Suppliers on pages 127-128.

Mending Torn Canvas

Needlepoint canvas should be handled gently. But even the most careful needleworker may have to cope with a torn canvas. If the canvas is worked in the area of the tear, pick out enough stitches to bare several mesh holes all around. If the tear occurs in an unworked area, stitch several lines around it. Pull out the broken canvas threads both ways, and pull them through the stitches on the reverse side with a thin crochet hook. Remove a few canvas threads from the edge and, threading them through a needle, darn the hole by weaving vertically and horizontally. (Figure 4.) Fasten the tail ends into the worked canvas on the reverse side.

FIGURE 4

This method of mending canvas is applicable to *interwoven* canvas only. Interlocked canvas must be patched. To do this, cut a piece of canvas large enough to extend 1" all around the torn area. Trim the hole into an even square or rectangle. Place the patch under the opening, being careful to line up all the meshes. Baste with thread that matches the canvas and work through both pieces, extending about 1" around the damaged part. Cut away any excess on the other side.

Yarns

Needlepoint yarns come in a wide variety of colors and textures. The yarns used in canvas work must be strong enough to withstand the pull through the canvas without fraying.

Persian yarn is the most popular and practical needlepoint yarn. It is all wool and is available in an enormous selection of colors. Persian yarn is made of three strands (plies), which separate easily and may be adapted to any size mesh by adding or removing one or more plies. Subtle shadings can be achieved by blending two or more shades.

English crewel is also a multi-ply wool yarn. It is somewhat thinner than the Persian type and may require an extra strand of yarn to cover a given canvas.

Tapestry yarn is a four-ply twist that does not separate into single plies. It is excellent for any needlework but only fits some canvas gauges, usually # 10 and sometimes # 12. Pre-test on a piece of canvas before beginning a large project.

Rug yarn is the heaviest of all and will cover rug canvas such as # 3, # 4, and # 5.

Silk is one of the most beautiful needlepoint materials. The English silk is a little more shiny than the French, and it has a tendency to fray. French silk has a beautiful satin luster and is very nice to work with. Add small amounts of silk for highlights and a touch of elegance.

Six-strand embroidery floss is a soft and manageable cotton thread that comes in many colors and may be used to highlight small areas. It soils easily and should not be worked over a large area, unless the needlework is washable.

There are a number of needlepoint yarns made from synthetic fibers. They do not come in as many colors as wool yarns, and they have a tendency to mat after a time. However, they are washable, non-allergic, and often less expensive than wool.

Tools and Supplies

Needles. Needles come in a large variety of specialized shapes and sizes. They are divided into two general categories: sharp-pointed, such as crewel and darners for work on densely woven fabrics, and blunt-pointed (tapestry) needles for open weaves such as canvas or net. Needles must be compatible with both the fabric and the working yarns. Purchase them by size (gauge). The finer the needle the larger its number. Needles are distributed under different brand names, and although the eye gauge is fairly constant, the length of the shaft may vary. Find the length that is most comfortable in your hand.

Thimbles. Thimbles are a matter of personal preference. Some needles slide through canvas so easily that it is not always necessary to use a thimble. But if you use one, select one that fits comfortably.

Scissors. Two pairs of scissors are a must: one small, sharp-pointed pair that fits into small areas to rip stitches or to cut yarn ends; and a large pair to cut canvas and other fabric.

Tape. Tape is another necessity. It should be the self-adhesive masking tape available in hardware stores. A 1" width is adequate. Fold it over the cut edge of the canvas to prevent the threads from raveling and to make the canvas easier to handle.

A **ruler** or measuring tape should also be part of your needlework "tool box," as well as some fine-point acrylic **marking pens**, and a small **magnet** to pick up stray pins and needles.

SLANTED STITCHES

This book is an introduction to the slanted stitch and stitch patterns used in needlepoint. The basic slanted stitch is the Half-Cross which is placed over the *crossover* (intersection) point of the horizontal and vertical canvas mesh.

All of the stitches described in this book are derived from this slanted or diagonal line. Each stitch or stitch pattern is shown in graph outline and photographic detail. Study and practice them individually or in combination with other stitches in order to understand their properties and construction.

Practice stitch patterns on single-mesh as well as double-mesh canvas. Work double mesh in large stitches (gros point), or separate the two threads and work in small stitches (petit point). (Figure 5.)

Blend colors in small patterns, and keep a file of stitches for future reference.

Half-Cross Stitch

There are three separate stitch techniques used in working the simple diagonal line stitch: the Half-Cross Stitch, Tent (or Continental), and the Basketweave.

The Half-Cross Stitch technique should be worked from left to right and right to left on double-thread canvas as indicated in the stitch detail in Figure 6. The stitches are placed diagonally across the canvas, and the needle is carried under the canvas in a vertical position.

This technique does not distort the canvas as much as the Continental Stitch, but its coverage isn't as good. It is generally used as a first row in Cross Stitch. Alternating rows of Half-Cross Stitch and Continental Stitch technique will form a series of horizontal ridges that can add interest to an otherwise monotonous background.

FIGURE 5

Four types of slanted stitches worked on double-thread canvas: A, Continental Stitch, gros point; B, Continental Stitch, petit point; C and D, Diagonal Cross Stitch in different gauges.

FIGURE 6 Half Cross Stitch Detail

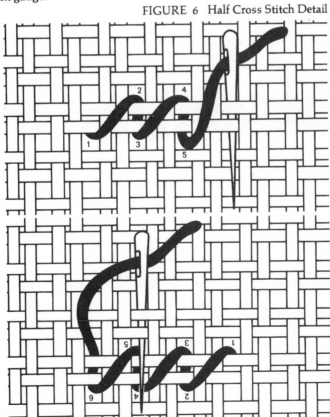

Tent (Continental) Stitch

The Tent is the smallest needlepoint stitch. It is also the most widely used because it adapts to intricate outlines and gives a smooth, flat, coverage. This is especially useful for work on painted needlepoint canvases when the design has to be faithfully reproduced.

The Tent is the basic slanted stitch worked over one intersection of a vertical and horizontal canvas thread. (Figures 7 and 8.) The stitch is always worked from lower left to upper right. The needle comes up at 1, goes in at 2, comes up at 3, and goes in at 4. Continue the line, working from right to left. At the end of the row, complete the last stitch and turn the canvas completely around. Work each row from right to left, and turn canvas around before beginning a new row. Study the stitch detail and practice the Tent Stitch horizontally, diagonally, and vertically. The needle motion is indicated in numbers.

The Tent Stitch will distort canvas and thus requires blocking. Learn to work the Basketweave technique, and use the Tent for vertical or horizontal lines and general outlines. (Figure 9.)

FIGURE 9 (See color page C3, Bottom, D)

FIGURE 7 Continental Stitch Detail

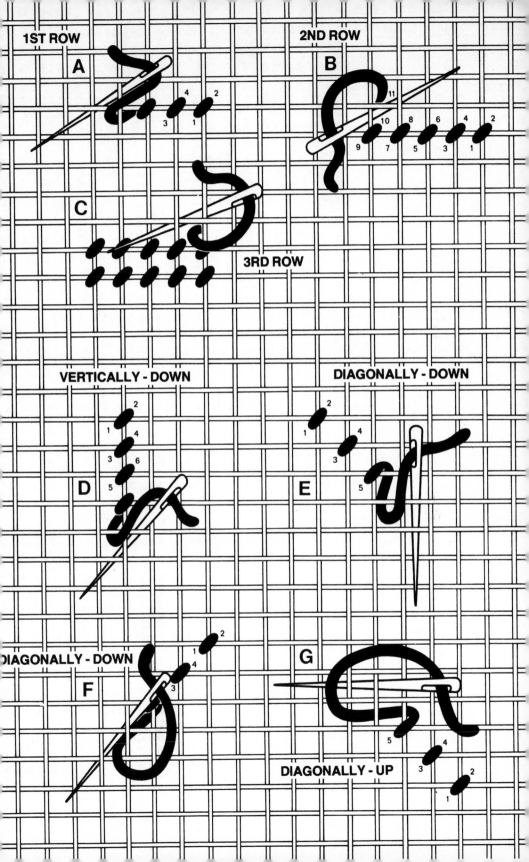

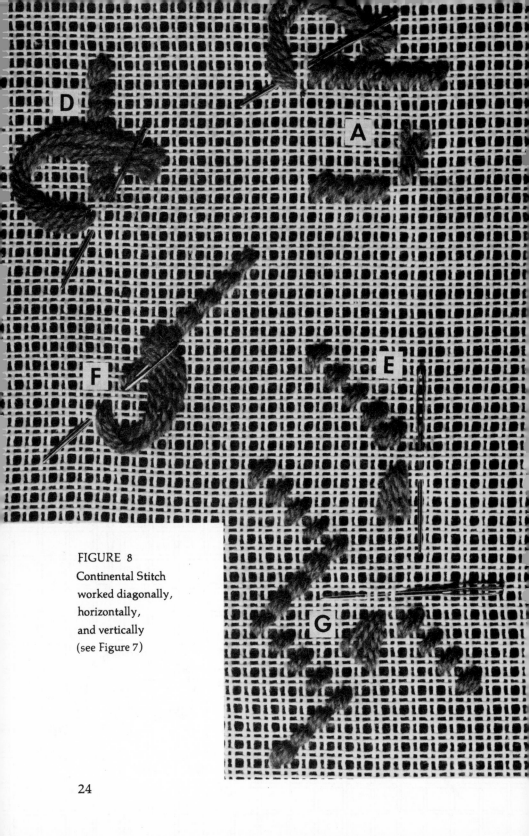

FIGURE 8
Continental Stitch
worked diagonally,
horizontally,
and vertically
(see Figure 7)

24

Basketweave (Diagonal Tent) Stitch

The Basketweave is worked in diagonal rows across the canvas. The first stitch is placed at the top right-hand corner of the section to be covered. The second stitch is placed to the left of the first, and the third stitch is placed directly below the first. (The sequence of the last two stitches is interchangeable.)

From this point, the stitches are worked in diagonal lines from lower right to upper left with the needle held in a horizontal position, and returned from upper left to lower right with the needle in a vertical position. (Figure 10.)

Figure 11 illustrates a progression of twenty-five stitches forming a square. Practice this sample in sequence exactly as shown. Watch the position of the needle as you work the diagonal rows. It is this constant changing of position that creates the interwoven (Basketweave) texture on the reverse side.

This weave gives the needlework durability and prevents the distortion so common in diagonal stitches. Special care must be taken to alternate the direction of the diagonal rows. Two rows worked in the same direction will create a permanent ridge in the texture of the work.

Before putting the work aside, leave a row unfinished with the needle in the proper position. When you resume work, there will be less likelihood of making an error.

Although the Basketweave is only a special way to work a Half-Cross Stitch, the overall texture differs. The stitches lift and twist slightly and occasionally require an extra strand of yarn to cover the canvas. The Continental, or Tent, is more even and smooth. Both may be used on the same canvas in separate design areas but not interchangeably. For example, a center design may be worked in Tent Stitches and the background material finished in Basketweave to minimize distortion. Check your gauge for coverage.

The sample in Figure 12 is worked in Basketweave.

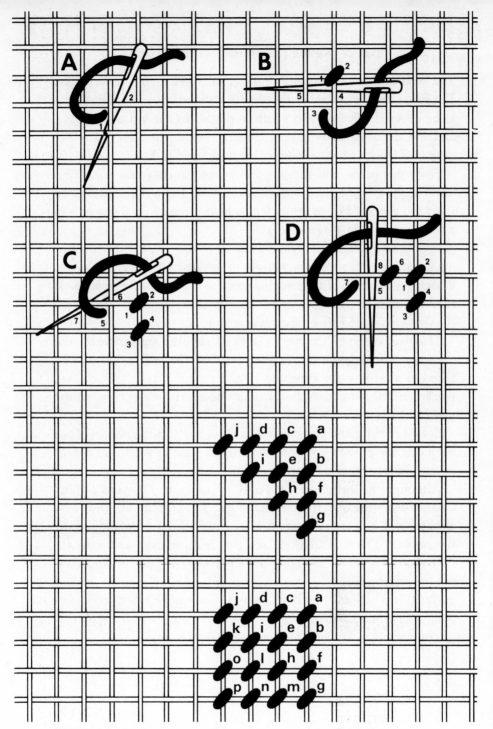

FIGURE 10 Basketweave Stitch Detail

FIGURE 11
Basketweave Stitch Progression

26

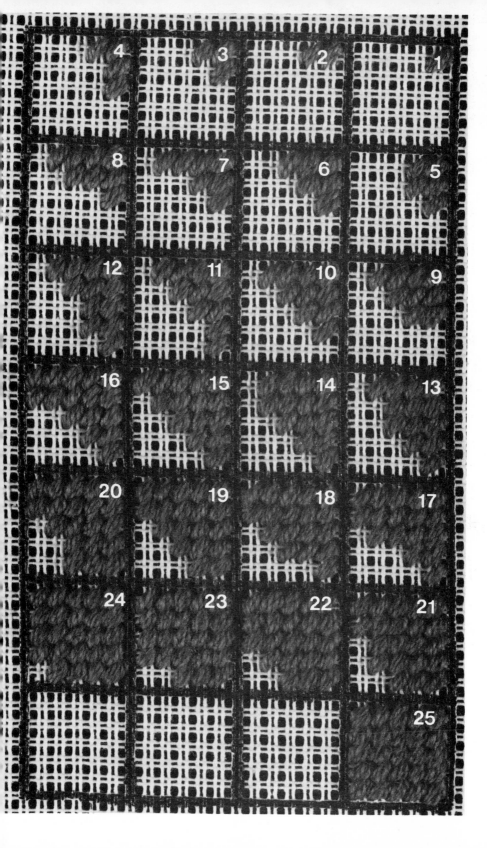

FIGURE 12
(See color page C3, Bottom, C)

28

Slanting (Oblique) Gobelin Stitch

The Slanting Gobelin Stitch is a large Tent Stitch worked diagonally over two or more canvas threads. It is the foundation stitch for all the slanted stitch patterns. The Slanting Gobelin is worked in straight rows, and the first and last stitches are compensated with Tent Stitches to straighten the outline. Compensating stitches are stitches that have to be shortened or adjusted to fit in odd places or to straighten out a margin line.

Study Figures 13 and 14, and practice several rows of Slanting Gobelin in various gauges. Compare its texture and coverage with that of the Continental Stitch.

Work from right to left. At the end of the rows, turn canvas around and again work right to left.

FIGURE 13 Slanting Gobelin Stitches

29

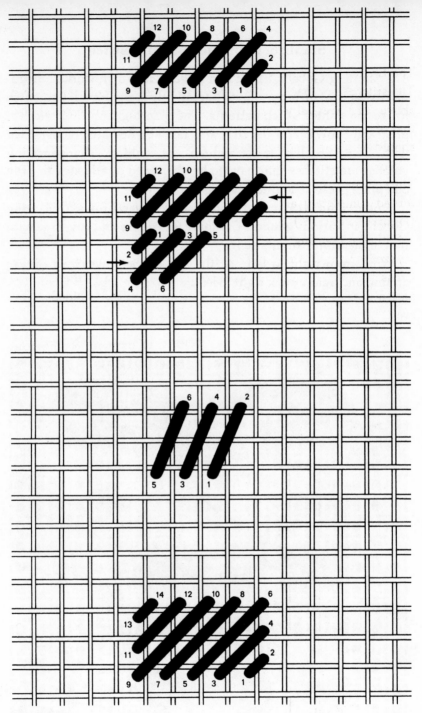

FIGURE 14
Slanting Gobelin Stitch Detail

Encroaching Gobelin

The Encroaching Gobelin is a variation of the Slanting Gobelin. The stitches encroach, or overlap, one canvas thread into the row above. The over-all texture of the Encroaching Gobelin resembles that of tapestry. It is an excellent background for shading, but it should be framed because it distorts the canvas.

Work stitches in an over-and-under motion from right to left. The return may be worked from left to right, or the canvas can be turned completely around and again worked from right to left. (Figures 15 and 16.)

Both the slanting and encroaching Gobelins create a slightly stylized effect. Details are not as finely outlined as in the Half-Cross Stitch. A needlepoint finished in Gobelin has the appearance of an old tapestry. Very fine details should be avoided, however.

FIGURE 15
Encroaching Gobelin Stitch Detail

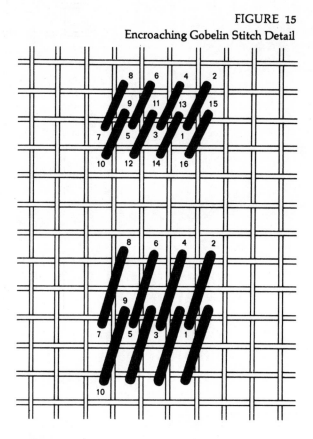

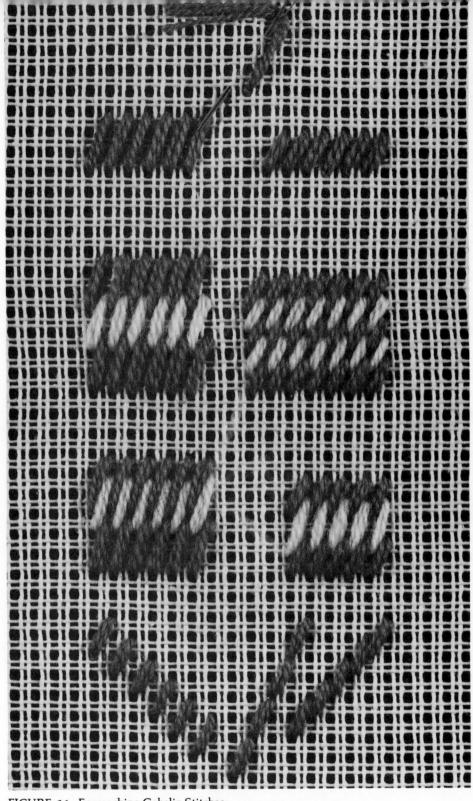

FIGURE 16 Encroaching Gobelin Stitches

Kelim (Kalem) Stitch

One way to counteract distortion in the Diagonal Stitch is to place another stitch on the adjoining line facing in the opposite direction. The Kelim is a Slanting Gobelin worked up and down in vertical rows. It is a texture rather than a stitch pattern.

There are two basic methods of working the Kelim. One is to bring the needle diagonally *under* the intersection of the horizontal and vertical canvas threads. (Figure 17, A.) At the end of each line, the needle goes across in a horizontal line to begin the next row in the opposite direction.

The Kelim can also be worked by carrying the thread diagonally across and up over a canvas square and then bringing the needle in a horizontal line under the canvas thread. (Figure 17, B.) When the vertical line is completed, the needle is carried across two canvas threads and the stitches are worked in reverse, meeting like chevrons.

Figure 18 shows the Kelim Stitch worked on double-mesh canvas.

Kelim Stitches form an interesting ridged texture. The various gauges that may be worked in this texture are illustrated in Figure 19.

A counted-stitch or a painted canvas may be translated into Kelim. Work in vertical lines instead of the horizontal or diagonal lines of the Tent. The diagonal lines must continue unbroken, alternating the upward and downward direction. Work up a horizontal row at the top of the design to line up the stitch direction. (Figure 18, C.)

FIGURE 17 Kelim Stitch Detail

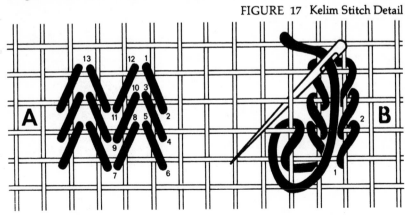

33

FIGURE 18 Kelim Stitch Detail and Stitches

FIGURE 19
Kelim Stitch Variations

Slanted Stitch Patterns

A combination of two or more line stitches that form a specific pattern and easily identified texture is called a stitch pattern, or stitch formation. Some textures are achieved with a particular stitch technique, that is, single stitches worked in close formation in vertical, horizontal, or diagonal lines.

The only true patterns in the slanted stitch series are the Mosaic, Cashmere, and Scotch Stitch patterns, and the Cross Stitch variations. The Mosaic, Cashmere, and Scotch have the same basic construction—beginning with a Tent Stitch, continuing with a number of Slanting Gobelin Stitches, and ending with a Tent Stitch. (Figure 20.)

FIGURE 20
Progression of Slanted Stitch Patterns

Mosaic Stitch Pattern

The Mosaic is the smallest of the slanted stitch patterns. It consists of three stitches and is worked like the Continental from right to left, diagonally or horizontally. Complete one unit at a time. (Figures 21 and 22.)

The Mosaic may be used to enlarge a counted-stitch pattern (one Moasic pattern is equivalent to four Tent Stitches in counted space). The red and white design shown in Figure 99 and on color page C2 is worked entirely in Mosaic.

FIGURE 21   Mosaic Stitch Detail

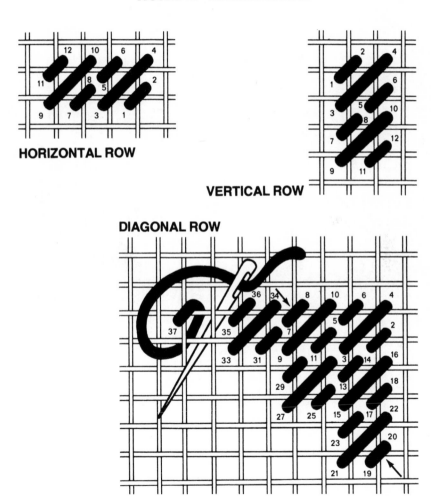

HORIZONTAL ROW

VERTICAL ROW

DIAGONAL ROW

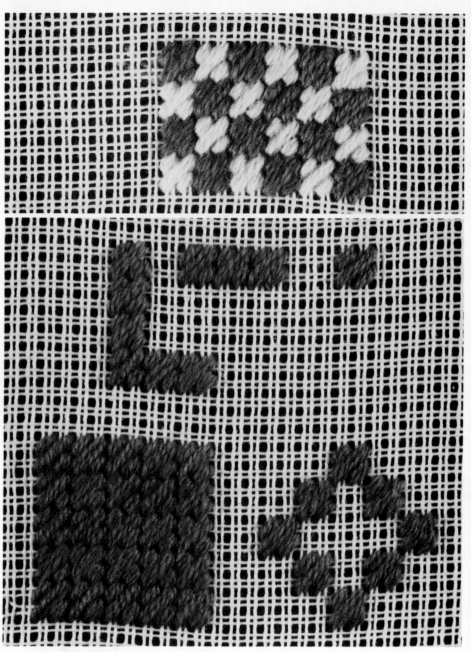

FIGURE 22
Mosaic Stitch Patterns

Scottish (Scotch) Stitch Pattern

The Scottish Stitch (also known as Flat Stitch and Diagonal Satin) is a larger version of the Mosaic Stitch pattern. It begins with the Tent Stitch and continues with a series of two or more progressively longer Gobelin Stitches. After the longest stitch is placed, the rest of the stitches are decreased until they end with a Tent Stitch. (Figure 23.)

The Scottish Stitch pattern is usually square. It adapts to a number of variations and may be enclosed in a framework of Tent Stitches as indicated in Figures 24 and 25.

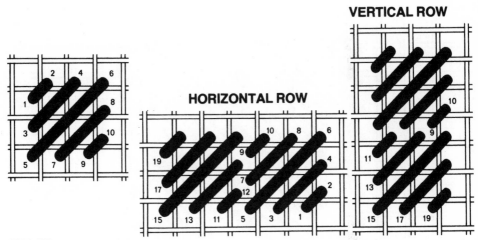

FIGURE 23
Scottish Stitch Detail and Pattern

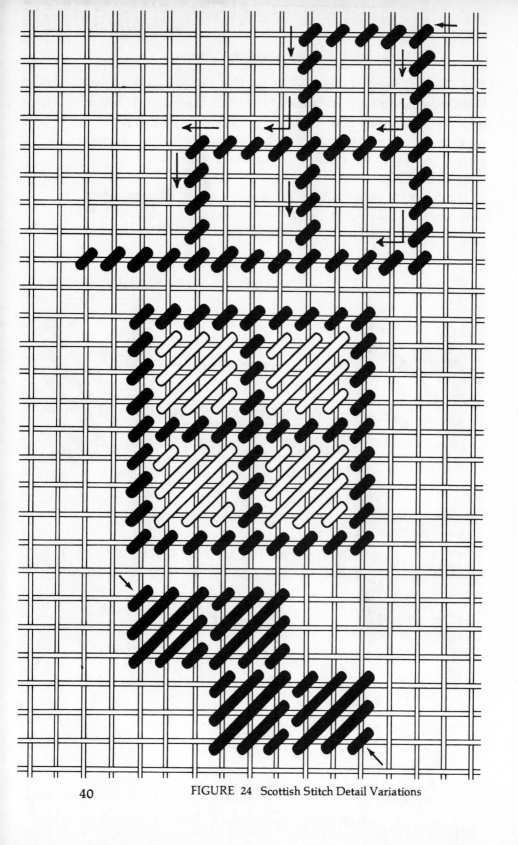

FIGURE 24 Scottish Stitch Detail Variations

FIGURE 25   Scottish Stitch Detail Variations

Cushion Stitch Pattern

The Cushion Stitch pattern is another variation of the Scottish. These stitch patterns are worked in diagonal rows, with a large stitch placed between the two Tent Stitches. Study the framework in Figure 26. The large stitch is worked in a second color to make it more visible, but it is a continuation of the stitch construction. Work diagonal rows of Scottish Stitch patterns interspersed with a long stitch that is twice the width of the center Gobelin.

Complete the pattern by covering the long dividing stitch with a diagonal row (in reverse) of Scottish patterns. The stitch patterns converge at a center point and counter-balance the distortion. They create an attractive quilted texture in geometric designs.

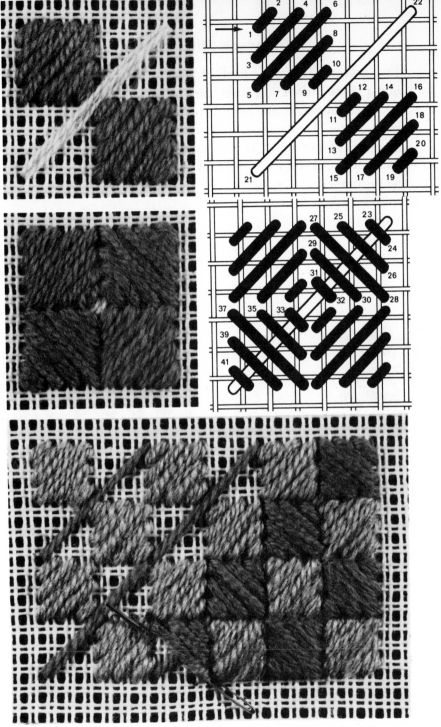

FIGURE 26 Cushion Stitch Detail and Patterns

Cashmere Stitch Pattern

The Cashmere is similar to the Mosaic Stitch pattern. It begins with a Tent Stitch but continues with two or more Gobelin Stitches of identical size before ending with the last Tent Stitch. For an over-all Cashmere texture, don't work more than two Gobelin Stitches per unit. The Cashmere is highly distortive and should not be used over large areas unless the finished needlework will be framed or upholstered. (Figures 27 and 28.)

FIGURE 27
Cashmere Stitch Detail

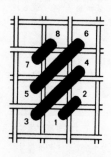

HORIZONTAL ROW

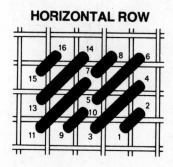

VERTICAL ROW

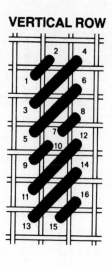

DIAGONAL ROW

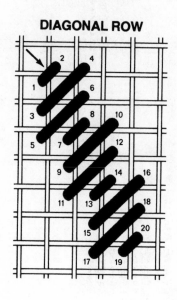

FIGURE 28
Cashmere Stitch Pattern

Checks (Chequer) Stitch Pattern

The Check pattern is a combination of Mosaic or Scottish Stitch units worked alternately with groups of Tent Stitches for an interesting change in texture.

Work in diagonal lines to minimize distortion. The Scotch or Mosaic patterns begin at lower right and are carried to the upper left. (Figures 29 and 30.) The Tent Stitch should be worked in the diagonal Tent or Basketweave.

The Chequer is very striking when worked in a monochromatic combination of matte and shiny yarns.

FIGURE 29 Check Stitch Pattern

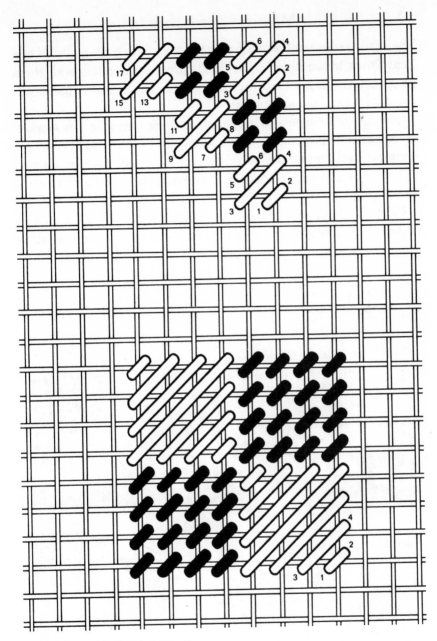

FIGURE 30 Check Stitch Detail

Milanese Stitch Pattern

The Milanese resembles half of a Scottish Stitch. Begin with one Tent Stitch in the lower right-hand corner, and follow with three progressively larger Gobelin Stitches. Do not increase, but begin again with the Tent and repeat.

The row of Milanese is diagonal, and the return row is worked in the opposite direction in a different color or shading. It creates a textured background and may be used by itself to cover a small pillow or handbag. It adds an interesting texture to patchwork items. (Figure 31.)

When the Milanese Stitch pattern is worked within a square or rectangular framework, it needs a number of compensating stitches to fit into the corners and narrow spaces. (Figure 32.)

FIGURE 32 Milanese Stitch Pattern

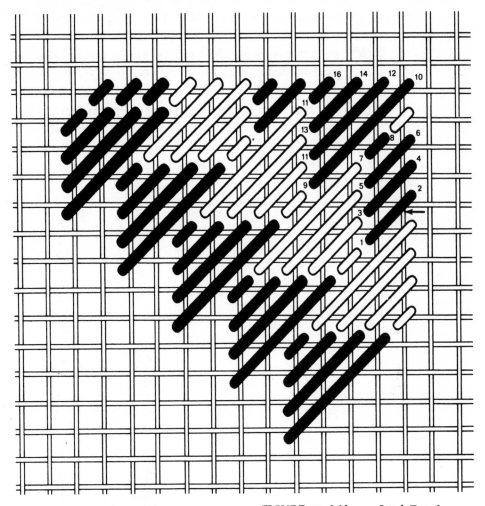

FIGURE 31 Milanese Stitch Detail

Byzantine Stitch Pattern

The Byzantine is actually a texture, not a stitch pattern. It is worked in a series of steps in diagonal rows. The steps are Slanting Gobelin Stitches that alternate in vertical and horizontal lines.

Begin at the bottom right corner with a Tent Stitch, and continue as for the Scottish pattern. When you reach the longest Gobelin Stitch, continue working the same length in vertical and horizontal rows as indicated in Figures 33 and 34.

Place the first Byzantine row through the center of the area to be covered. This will create a guideline above and below the row of stitches. The Byzantine has a strong, highly visible texture and should be used carefully lest it overpower other stitch patterns. It creates attractive zigzag lines that may be shaded or worked in contrasting colors. The width of the stitches may vary.

Note: The Byzantine distorts the fabric and it might need some blocking.

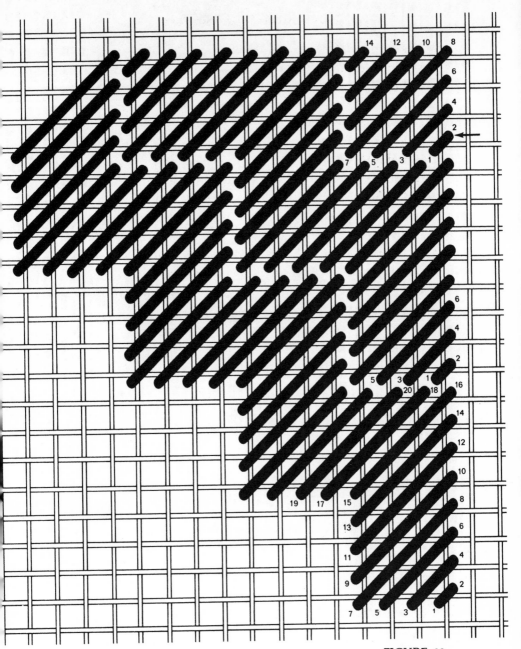

FIGURE 33
Byzantine Stitch Detail

51

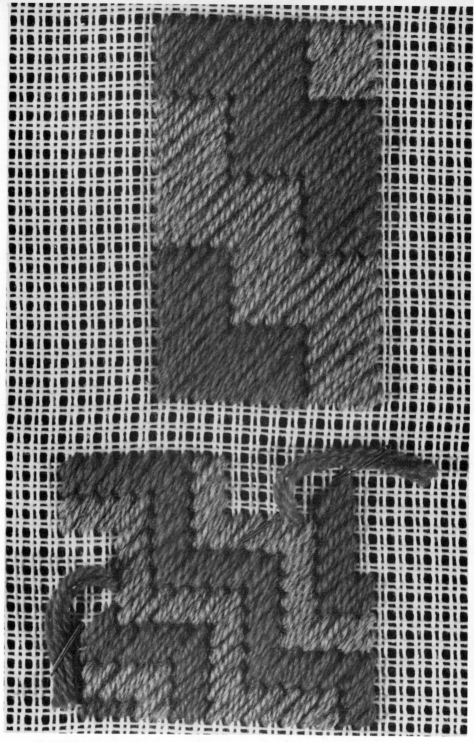

FIGURE 34 Byzantine Stitch Patterns

Jacquard Stitch Pattern

The Jacquard is another texture created with a specific stitch placement. It is worked exactly as the Byzantine Stitch pattern except that the wide Gobelin Stitches alternate with Tent Stitches. Since the structure of the Tent Stitch is different from the Gobelin, watch the stitches as they turn direction from a horizontal line to a vertical one. (Figures 35 and 36.)

FIGURE 36 Jacquard Stitch Pattern

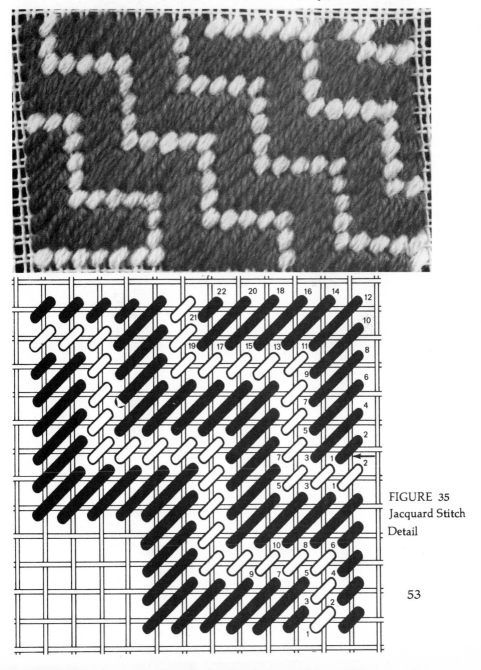

FIGURE 35
Jacquard Stitch
Detail

53

Running Stitch, Back Stitch, and Stem Stitch

The Running Stitch, Back Stitch, and Stem Stitch may be worked in a slanted line and can be very effective on open-mesh canvas in evenly counted spaces. (Figures 37, 38, and 39.)

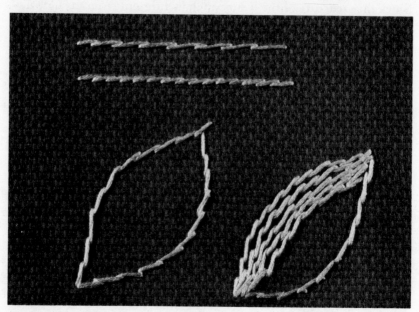

FIGURE 38 Stem Stitch

FIGURE 37
Stem Stitch Detail

FIGURE 39
A, Back Stitch Detail;
B, Running Stitch Detail
(diagonal versions)

Cross Stitch Patterns and Textures

Another way to counteract the distortion of the diagonal sitch is to criss-cross the stitches. This creates a Cross Stitch pattern. The Cross Stitch patterns may be finished as individual units or worked as Half-Cross stitches in one row and crossed over on the return row.

The Cross Stitch does not distort canvas and is an excellent choice for needlepoint rugs. The extra thickness it provides makes the finished work firmer and more durable. Work all Cross Stitch patterns on double-thread or interlocked canvas.

There are a number of Cross Stitches that form individual patterns or textures and they can be worked in endless combinations of colors and gauges. They are all slanted stitches.

The simplest is the small diagonal Cross Stitch pattern. Design outlines worked in Cross Stitch patterns are more geometric than those worked in Tent Stitch. (Figures 40 and 41.)

The Cross Stitch pattern is worked on double-mesh or interlocked canvas.

The Oblong Cross Stitch is a variation sometimes known as the Long-Legged Cross Stitch. It is worked in the same way as the small Cross but over a larger number of canvas threads. (Figure 42.)

A number of variations are illustrated in Figure 43, including a line of crosses worked over a ribbon in contrasting color.

The Long-armed Cross Stitch creates a tightly woven texture that is often used for rug backgrounds. Study the four-step stitch detail. (Figures 44 and 45.) The needle comes up at odd numbers and goes back down at even numbers.

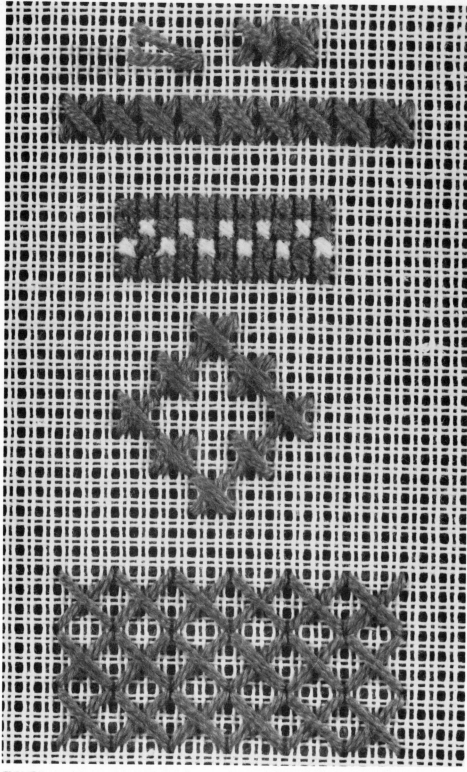

FIGURE 41 Cross Stitch Patterns

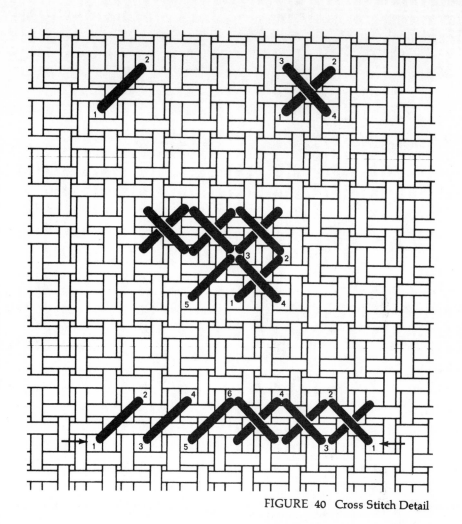

FIGURE 40 Cross Stitch Detail

FIGURE 42
Oblong Cross Stitch Detail

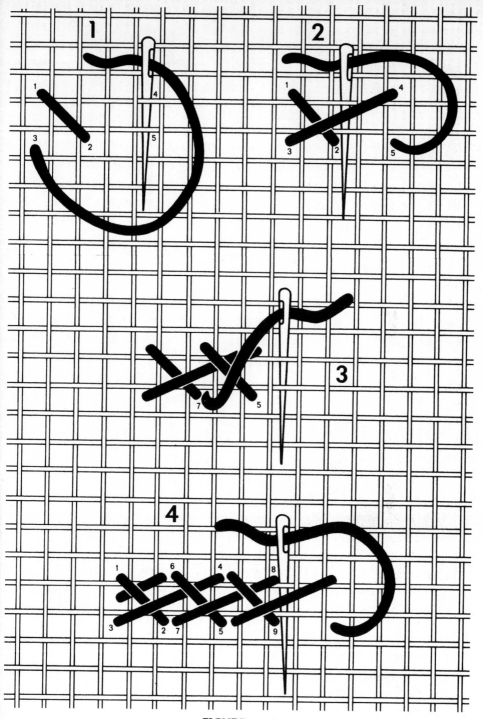

FIGURE 44 Long-armed Cross Stitch Detail

FIGURE 43

Oblong Cross Stitch Variations

59

FIGURE 45 Long-armed Cross Stitch Variations

60

Fern Stitch Pattern

The Fern is a type of Cross Stitch worked in vertical lines. Like the rest of the Cross Stitch patterns, it may be worked widely spaced with the fabric showing through, or as a tight texture covering the entire background.

Begin with a small Cross at the top to compensate for the wide gap, and work the stitch lines as indicated in Figure 46. The threaded needle comes up at odd numbers and goes in at even numbers in sequence. Notice that the stitches are spaced across five canvas squares at the top line and across three canvas squares at the bottom.

When the Fern Stitch Pattern is worked in close formation with a heavy yarn, it forms a textured plait down the center, which may be used for interesting design constructions. (Figure 47.)

FIGURE 46   Fern Stitch Detail

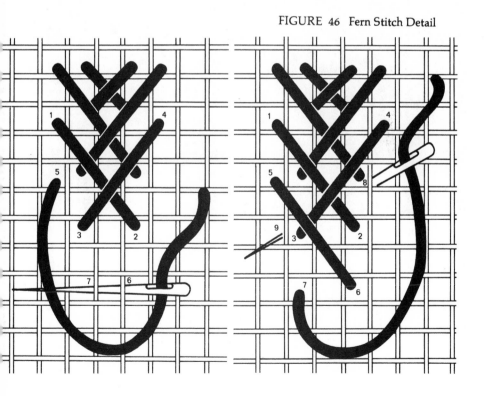

FIGURE 47
Fern Stitch Variations

Web Stitch Pattern

The Web begins on a foundation of the Scottish Stitch pattern. The base square is worked from top left to bottom right or in reverse. The square can be formed with any number of stitches. Place small Half-Crosses at the intersection of the canvas threads and work with heavy threads to prevent the canvas from showing through. This is a good fill-in stitch for patchwork or large design areas. The Cross Stitches begin at lower right. (Figures 48 and 49.)

FIGURE 48
Web Stitch Detail

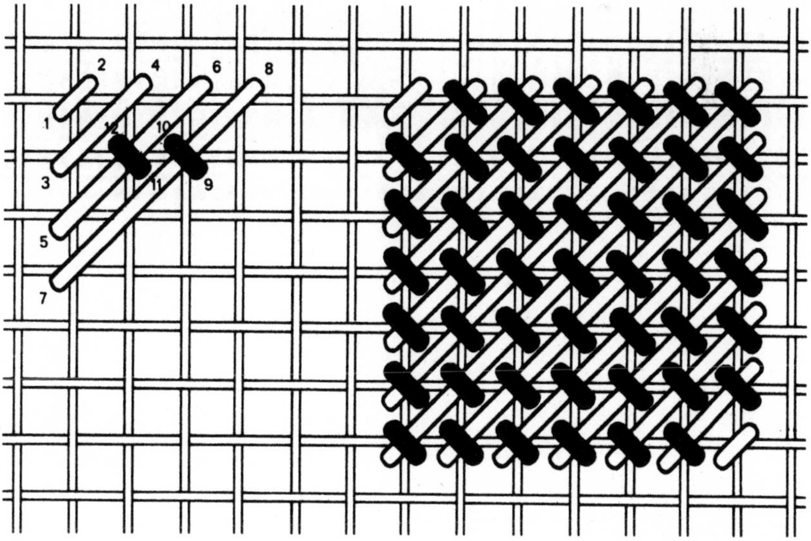

63

FIGURE 49
Web Stitch Pattern

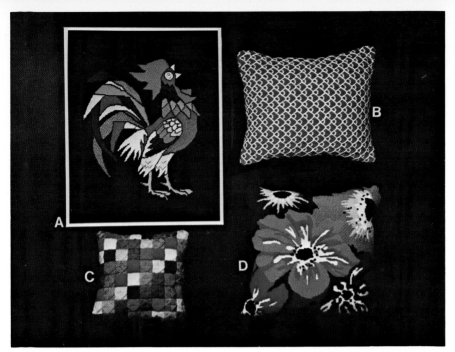

Top: A, Harlequin Rooster (Figures 69 and 70); B, Pillow worked in 10-color Herringbone (Figure 56); C, Pillow worked in Norwich Stitch (Figures 60 and 61); D, Pillow with Poppy design worked in Basketweave (Figure 102).

Bottom: A, Tennis Racquet Cover with Sneakers (Figure 96); B, Bokara Design (Figure 98); C, Handbag (courtesy Toni Totes, Inc.) with Woven Ribbon Design (Figures 80, 84, and 85); D, Pillow worked in Two-color Floral Design (Figure 99).

Top: Eagle design courtesy Alice Peterson (Figure 100); B, Tricycle Seat Cover —design © Downe Publishing, Inc. Reprinted by permission of Ladies' Home Journal Needle & Craft—designed by Elise Silverstein (Figure 71).

Bottom: A, Vest (courtesy America Hurrah) design by La Stitcherie, B, Umbrella Case; C, Small Purses courtesy Toni Totes, Inc. (Figures 90 and 91); D, Four-way Medallion (Figure 65).

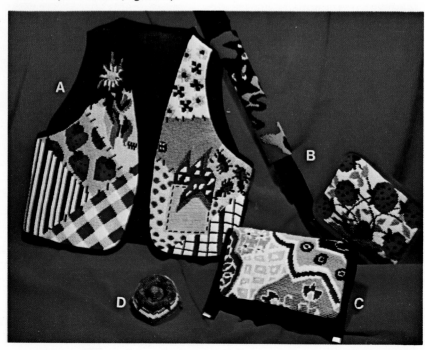

Top: A, Farmer and Farmer's Wife. Kit courtesy Toni Totes, Inc., finished dolls courtesy La Stitcherie; B, Beaver (Figure 95); C, Doll Pillow (Figure 97).

Bottom: A, Mondrian-style Distortion Project (Figure 68); B, Eye Glass Case design courtesy La Stitcherie; C, Eye Glass Case (Figure 12); D, Eye Glass Case (Figure 9); E, Handbag design courtesy La Stitcherie.

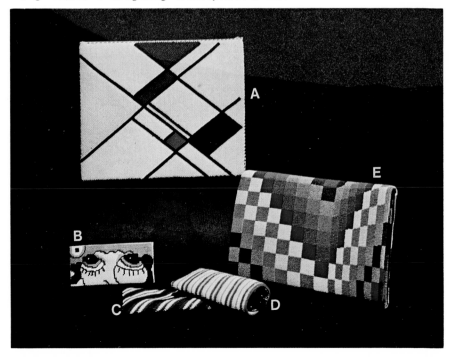

Leopards (Figure 101). Original design by Helen Maris.

Knotted Stitch

This is really a Cross Stitch that consists of one long Diagonal Gobelin crossed at the center with a small Half-Cross Stitch. Work from right to left, finishing each cross separately. Work the return row from left to right. (Figures 50 and 51.) This stitch creates a good tight background for rugs and chair seat covers.

FIGURE 50
Knotted Stitch Detail

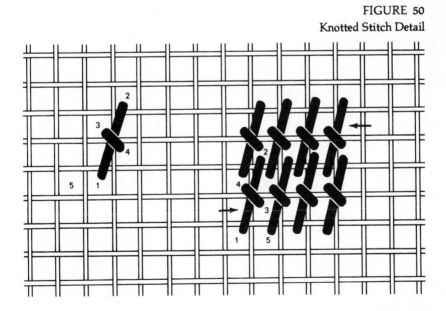

FIGURE 51 Knotted Stitch Pattern

Herringbone Stitch

The Herringbone is one of the most versatile of the Cross Stitches. It is worked open or closed and creates an attractive texture. The basic Herringbone Stitch is worked in a continuous motion from left to right, beginning at the top of the canvas. (Figure 53.)

The threaded needle comes up at 1, goes in at 2, comes up at 3, back at 4, and so on. (Figure 54 illustrates a series of Herringbone samples in various color combinations.)

A second color is placed into the skipped space between the stitches and worked in exactly the same manner as the first row. Several spaces can be left between the stitches of the first row and a new color introduced into each space.

The second row of Herringbone begins at the left and is worked to the right. Leave the same number of spaces to be filled in with colors as you did in the row above. (Figure 55 illustrates a multi-stitch Herringbone design.)

Figure 56 shows the Herringbone worked with nine colors on Rya cloth. (See also color page C1.)

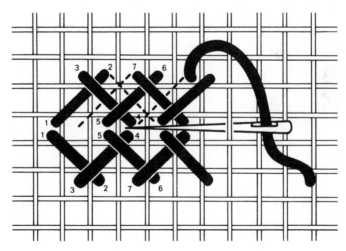

FIGURE 53
Herringbone Stitch Detail (dotted line indicates second color)

FIGURE 52
Four sample patterns worked in different diagonal stitches:
A, Kelim; B, Continental; C, Cross Stitch; D, Slanting Gobelin.

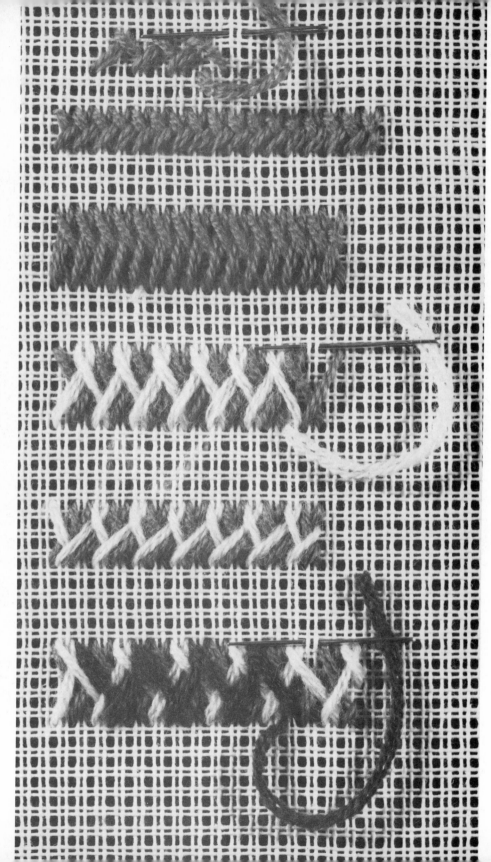

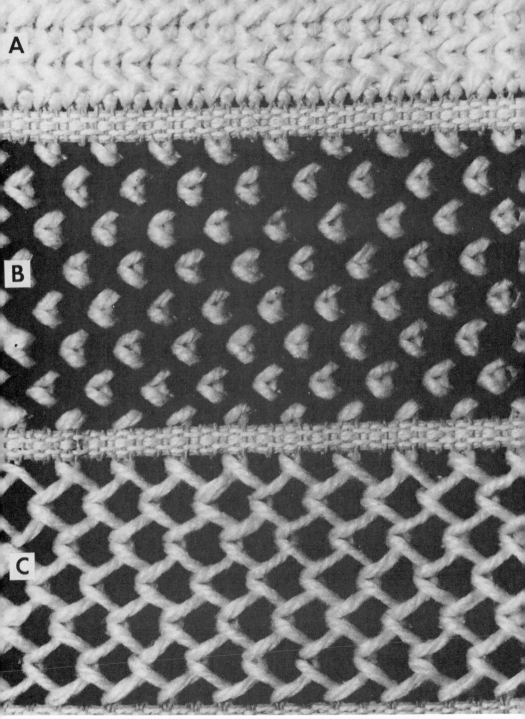

FIGURE 55 Herringbone Stitch Variations worked on one pattern (Figure 53): A, one color; B, two colors, dark predominating; C, two colors, light predominating.

FIGURE 54
Herringbone Stitch Variations

69

FIGURE 56

Herringbone Stitch Pattern worked in nine colors. Stitch progression appears
from top to bottom. Work pattern in horizontal lines left to right, top to bottom,
one color at a time (see color page C1, Top, B).

70

Four-Way Herringbone Stitch Pattern

The Four-Way Herringbone is a large block stitch pattern with a raised texture. The stitch detail is not shown in graph outline but in a numbered grid. (Figure 57.) Begin at the center. The threaded needle comes up at the odd numbers and goes in at the even. The four numbers at the outside corners indicate the starting point of the adjacent stitch details.

As you work up one stitch pattern, you will notice the basic Herringbone Stitch technique. There will be large spaces between the stitch patterns. This is the nature of the Four-Way Herringbone construction. Leave the spaces open to emphasize the bold design of this handsome pattern.

Figure 58 shows two finished stitch patterns and the starting point of a third one. The top portion of Figure 58 shows the reverse side of the fabric.

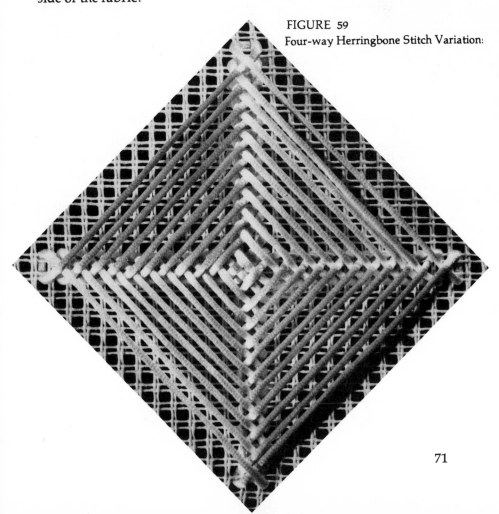

FIGURE 59
Four-way Herringbone Stitch Variation:

Work the Four-Way Herringbone in assorted colors or in one dark shade over a cream-colored background. Or create one large single pattern in shiny cord or heavy string on # 3 canvas for an interesting contemporary design. (Figure 59.)

Note: Do not weave heavy cord or string ends into the reverse side of stitches. Simply tie the new length of cord to the old one on the reverse side, being careful not to bring the knot onto the right side of the work.

FIGURE 57

Four-way Herringbone Stitch Detail

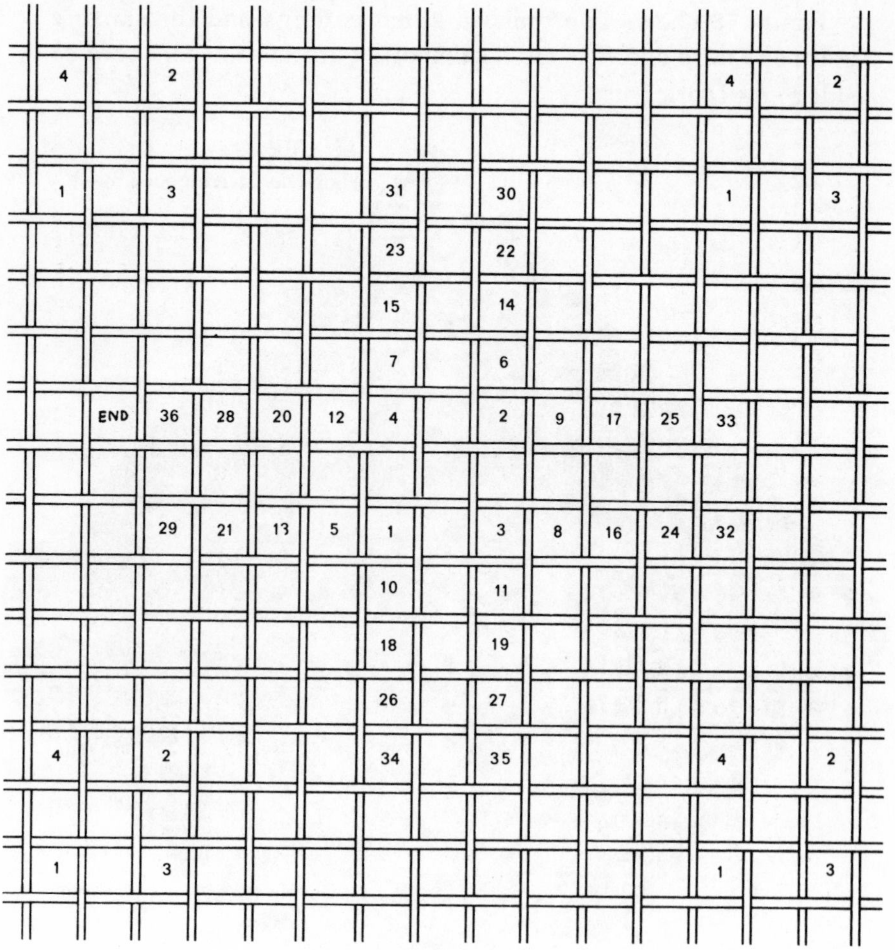

FIGURE 58 Four-way Herringbone Stitch Patterns

Norwich (Waffle) Stitch Pattern

The Norwich is a large textured stitch pattern that seems very complicated but can be easily mastered by following a stitch diagram. It is shown in a stitch-by-numbers diagram (Figure 60) as well as a twelve-step photograph (Figure 61).

The Norwich is worked over an odd number of canvas threads. It consists of a series of long diagonal stitches, which are worked clockwise. The stitches interlace on the top of the canvas and create only a border outline on the reverse side.

Come up at 1 and carry the needle across to 2; then go under to 3 and over to 4, and so on. Study the photograph as well as the stitch diagram. Work the stitches with lighter threads. On # 5 mesh canvas use only a three-ply Persian strand, and on # 10 use two or even one strand depending on the weight of the yarn. The stitches should not cross over on the reverse side. The last stitch is placed *under* the diagonal stitch immediately above it—i.e., in Figure 60, A, stitch 28 goes under stitch 21; and in Figure 60, B, stitch 36 is under 29.

The Norwich Stitch pattern, attractive in itself, may be worked in bold colors like patchwork (See color page C1) or in interesting geometric designs. (Figures 62 and 63.) To create a two-toned effect, work the first six steps in one color and the other six in a second color. For best results, use double-thread or interlocked canvas.

FIGURE 62

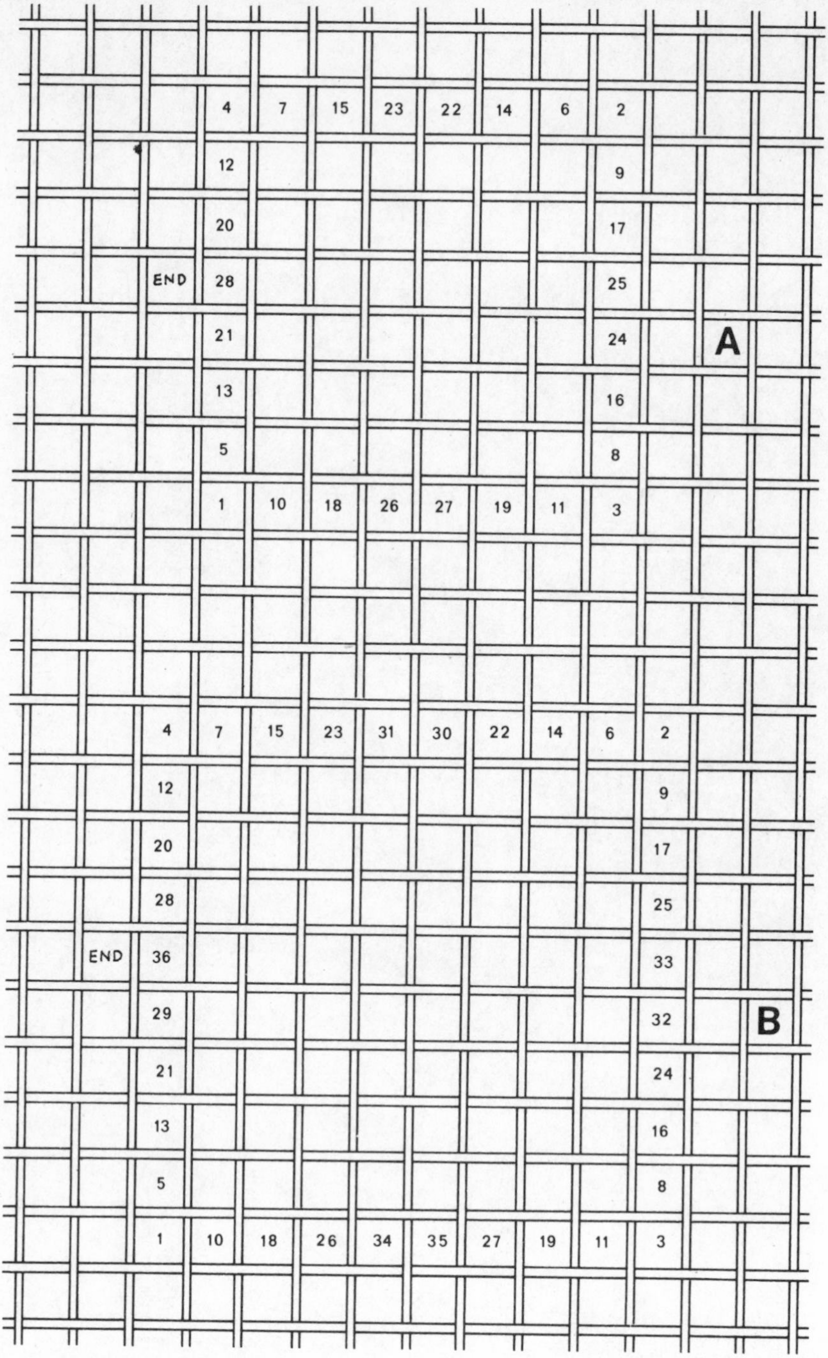

FIGURE 60 Norwich Stitch Detail

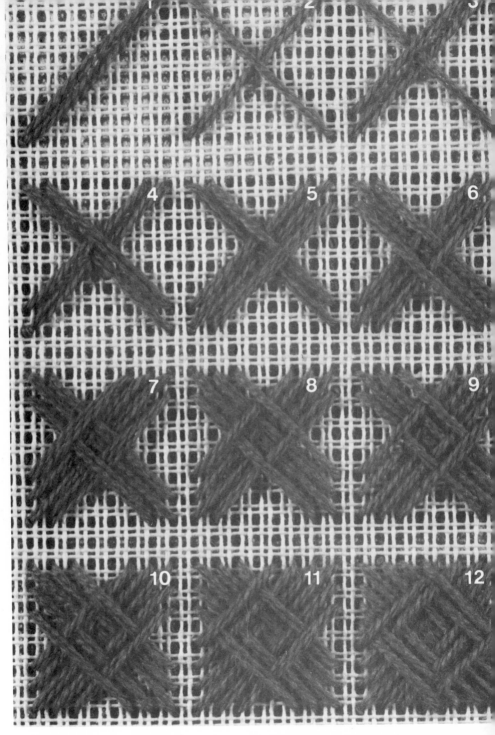

FIGURE 61   Norwich Stitch Progression (see color page C1, Top, C)

FIGURE 63

PROJECTS

Distortion In Slanted Stitches

Slanted needlepoint stitches worked in one direction will tend to distort the fabric. The distortion is more pronounced when the yarns are heavier than the fabric and the tension of the stitches is tight.

A number of techniques have been introduced over the years to relieve the distortion of the slanted stitches. The Basketweave technique is an improvement over the Half-Cross Stitches. An embroidery frame, where the threaded needle is carried up and down through the fabric rather than with a sideways tug, is also an improvement.

Slanting the stitches in two directions is the most widely used method of controlling distortion. Cross Stitch (page 55) is one method. Another is the Kelim Stitch (page 33) and its variations. Still another is placing blocks of slanted stitch patterns in opposite directions, thus counter-balancing the distortion. This is done with the Scotch, Cashmere, Mosaic, and other stitch patterns.

Distortion can at times become an asset and turn into attractive dimensional patterns. Study the samples in Figure 64. In Figure 64, A, two squares of equal size have been worked in the standard Tent Stitch. The canvas distortion is immediately evident.

When two more squares are worked in an opposite slant at the upper right and the lower left (Figure 64, B), the combined distortion squares the canvas and raises a dome in the center. This is an interesting design formation that has many possibilities for creating sculptured and three-dimensional projects. This is a four-way slanted stitch pattern which can be achieved only by working four squares in opposite directions. Mark the canvas to indicate the top and bottom, and work the stitches in this framework. If the can-

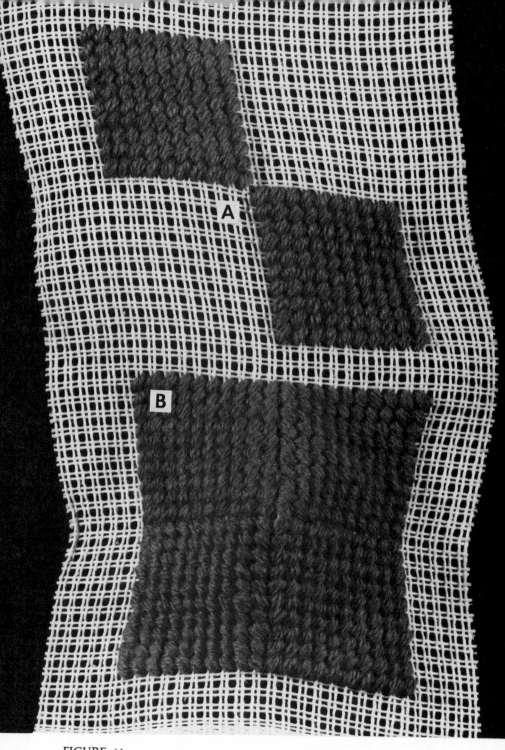

FIGURE 64

vas is turned sideways and one square worked in that position, the dome will not rise.

A number of designs may be adapted to this sculptured technique. Simply divide the canvas in four quarters by drawing a vertical and a horizontal line across the center. Work a four-way design, such as the one in Figure 65, or divide an attractive floral design into four squares. (Figure 66.) Always work the lower-right and the upper-left squares in the standard Tent Stitch (left to right). Reverse the stitch direction (right to left) at the upper-left and lower-right. Small designs may be used for jewelry. A large design becomes a striking sculptured wall hanging. (Figure 67.)

Experiment with other slanted stitches and stitch patterns. To add interest to a larger design, work several groups of Cross Stitches in a few areas. This will alter the dimension of the dome because Cross Stitches do not distort the fabric.

Another interesting distortion was created with a modern design outline. The square design (see color page C3) was turned and outlined as a diamond on the square canvas, and all the stitches were worked in standard Tent Stitch. The distortion simply changed the square into a rectangle, and it was left this way. (Figure 68.)

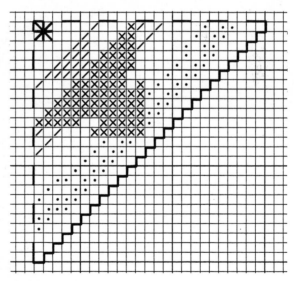

FIGURE 65

Diagram for Four-way Medallion (see color page C2, Bottom, D) ▪ = Yellow; ⊿ = Orange; ☒ = Green; ☐ = Purple.

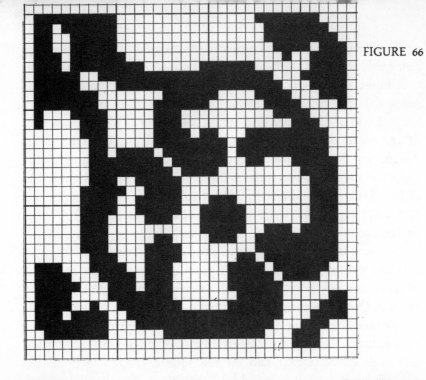

FIGURE 66

FIGURE 67

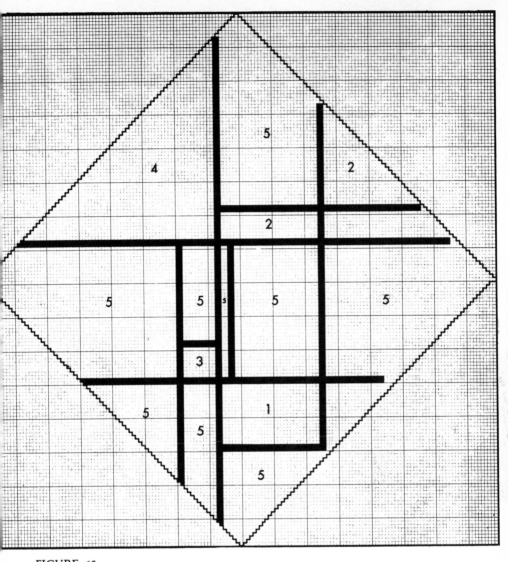

FIGURE 68
Graph for Mondrian-style pattern (see color page C3, Bottom, A).
2 = Blue; 3 = Red; 4 = Yellow; 5 = Bone or Beige.

Cutaway Or Waste Canvas

Open-mesh canvas is a fine background for counted-stitch and geometric designs that are not possible to work on conventional densely woven fabrics. However, a canvas can be stitched onto another fabric and the design worked through both layers as follows:

Place the portion of fabric to be embroidered on a frame or hoop. The frame should be large enough to accommodate the design with several inches to spare. Paint your design on a piece of single-mesh *interwoven* canvas that has been soaked in hot water, dried, and ironed flat.

Position the painted canvas over the fabric on the frame and pin in several places outside the work line. Then needlepoint the design, working through both layers of fabric. Use a sharp-pointed crewel rather than a blunt tapestry needle, and work each stitch in two motions: needle comes up, pull yarn—needle goes in, pull yarn.

When the work is finished, unpin the canvas and pull the warp and the weft threads from under the stitches. Do this gently, and if a thread resists, push back the stitches with the needle to find the trouble spot and clip with embroidery scissors to release it. This leaves the design on the fabric. Remove the work from the frame, and press. This method is used to decorate ties, velvet or denim clothing, and small decorative articles. The fabric should be heavy enough to support the weight of the canvas stitchery or it will buckle once the canvas threads are removed.

This method requires some expertise, and a beginner should attempt only a very small and simple pattern at first. Stitches must be very even, and special care must be taken not to snag the canvas. The proper tension can only be achieved through practice. If the tension is too loose, the stitches will lose their body when the canvas threads are pulled. If the tension is too tight, there might be some difficulty in pulling the threads.

There is a special canvas on the market, called waste canvas, designed especially for this method of stitching. It is a rather stiff, double-mesh that requires much soaking to remove the starch, and the mesh isn't as even as that of standard mono canvas.

Canvas used for cut-away projects should be completely free of sizing. A hot water soak *before* the needlepoint is applied will do the job. Soaking the needlepoint after it is finished is impractical. The fabric to be stitched may not be washable, and the paint media on the canvas might bleed a little. And any sizing residue that remains in the yarn will give it an unattractive stiffness.

Small pieces of interwoven canvas should be machine stitched around the edges to prevent excessive raveling. If several projects using the cut-away method are contemplated, soak a large square of canvas for several hours in hot water, roll it in a towel, and stretch it on a blocking board to restore the even weave. Press and keep flat, to be used as needed. If some stiffness remains, pull a canvas thread to see if it separates easily. If it offers too much resistance, wash it again.

A much simpler method of working with cut-away canvas is to use the *interlocked* type. This is a thin canvas with flat threads, which does not ravel and needs no pre-soaking. It remains on the fabric. Work the stitches to within one or two canvas threads at the edge of the design, cut the canvas very close to the outline, and place the last stitches over the edge and into the fabric. If canvas still shows around the margin, place an outline of back stitches in matching or contrasting color all around. This method may be applied to larger projects, eliminating the need for a needlepoint background.

The harlequin rooster shown in Figures 69 and 70 (color page C1) is worked in this manner on a background of black velvet.

Enlarge the rooster to any size, and outline it on # 10 or # 12 interlocked canvas. Stretch and staple a piece of black velvet or fabric of similar weight to a frame. Leave a margin allowance of at least 3" all around. Position the canvas over the fabric on the frame, and pin in several places to prevent shifting.

Beginning at center, work stitches in two motions through both layers of fabric, first the black outline and then the colors. It is possible to vary some of the stitches within the small patches. Stitch patterns such as the Cashmere, Milanese, Slanted Gobelin, or Kelim are interesting.

When the needlepoint is finished, cut away the canvas very close to the rooster outline. Use sharp-pointed scissors to get into the tight little corners, being careful not to nick the fabric. Work a second outline in the background around the rooster to cover any canvas that may show. Use Tent or Back Stitches for this.

If the fabric was nicked accidentally, glue a small piece of matching fabric to the underside and let dry before stitching the outline. If the fabric is stretched on a standard artist's frame, it can be mounted into a decorative frame as is. (See framing instructions on page 123.)

FIGURE 69
Graph for Harlequin Rooster. Black = Black; ◨ and 1 = Magenta; ◙ and 2 = Red-orange; 3 = Light orange; 4 = Gold; 5 = Yellow; 6 = Turquoise; 7 = Medium blue; 8 = Dark blue; 9 = Violet; 10 = Purple; 11 = Light green; 12 = Medium green.

FIGURE 70
Harlequin Rooster (see color page C1, Top, A)

Tricycle Seat Cover

(See color page C2.)

MATERIALS: One square of # 5 double-thread canvas to accommodate the entire outline of the tricycle seat cover plus a 2" margin all around.
20 yards each rug yarn in red, white, light blue, and medium blue.
1 yard rug yarn in black
3/4 yard denim or duck
1 yard cotton cord or shoe lace

Place a sheet of paper over the seat cover, and pencil in the outline. Fold the paper in half, lengthwise, and straighten the outline. Add 1" all around and trace on a square of canvas.

The lady bug is shown in actual size in Figure 71. Position the canvas over the design, and trace it. (See general tracing directions on page 11.)

Work the needlepoint in Diagonal Tent Stitch (Basketweave). The lady bug is outlined in black and filled in with red. The background is worked in a gingham pattern. (Figure 83.)

Place the finished canvas on top of the seat cover to check the over-all size, and add a few stitches all around if necessary.

Cut out the seat outline, leaving a 1" margin allowance. (Figure 72, A.) To finish, cut 4" strips diagonally across the denim, and machine stitch them end to end until they form one strip long enough to go around the seat cover outline. (Figure 72, B.) Fold over one edge about 1", and machine stitch along the fold, leaving a tubular opening of about 3/4".

Fasten the cord or shoe lace to a large safety pin. Slip the closed pin through this tubular opening (Figure 72, C), and pull it through the other end.

Pin the other edge of the denim strip along the outline of the seat cover, wrong sides together. Begin at the back and bring it all around, ending with a slight overlap. Pin into one row of stitches so that the bare canvas threads will not show at the seam.

Check the eveness of the outline and correct pins. Baste all around and remove pins. Finish with two rows of machine stitching, and then remove basting thread. (Figure 72, D.)

Turn the seat cover right-side out (Figure 72, E), slip over the tricycle seat, and pull the cord at both ends. Twist several times around the shaft underneath the seat, and tie securely.

FIGURE 71

Diagram for Tricycle Cover (see color page C2, Top, B)

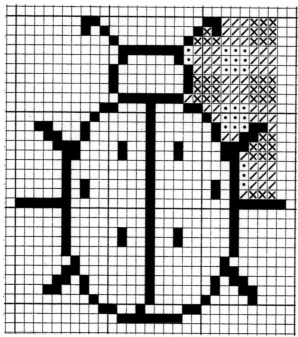

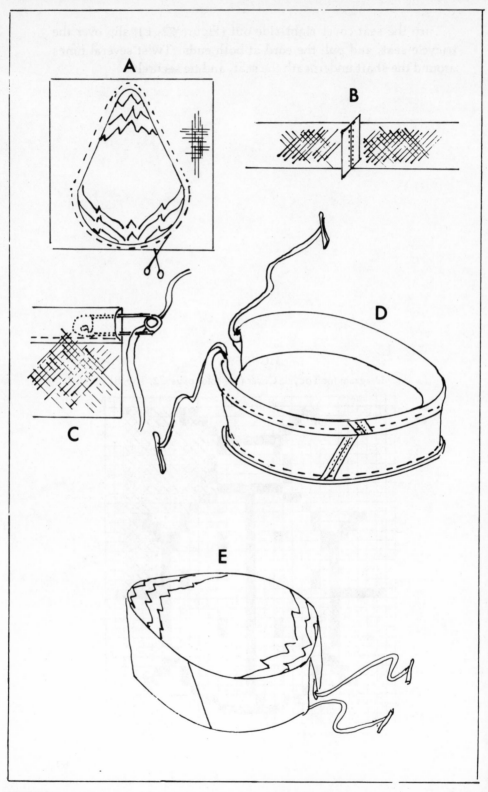

FIGURE 72

Alphabet

This alphabet may be worked in Continental or Cross Stitches. Letters need fifteen to twenty canvas meshes in each direction plus space between. Some of the letters are worked on a "tumbling block" background (see page 95). They are the first and last initials of the members of one family. (Figures 73 and 74.)

Note: Q=O and M=W inverted.

FIGURE 73

Alphabet suitable for Cross or Half-cross Stitch monograms. (W = M inverted; O = Q without tail).

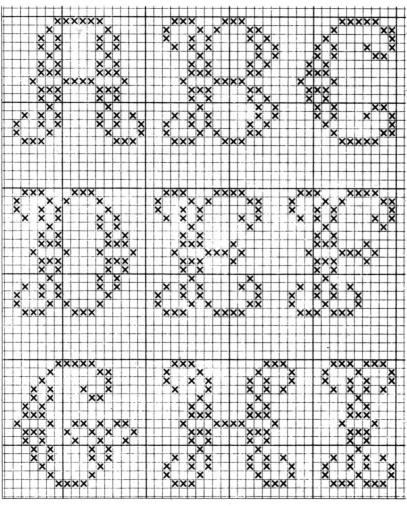

FIGURE 74

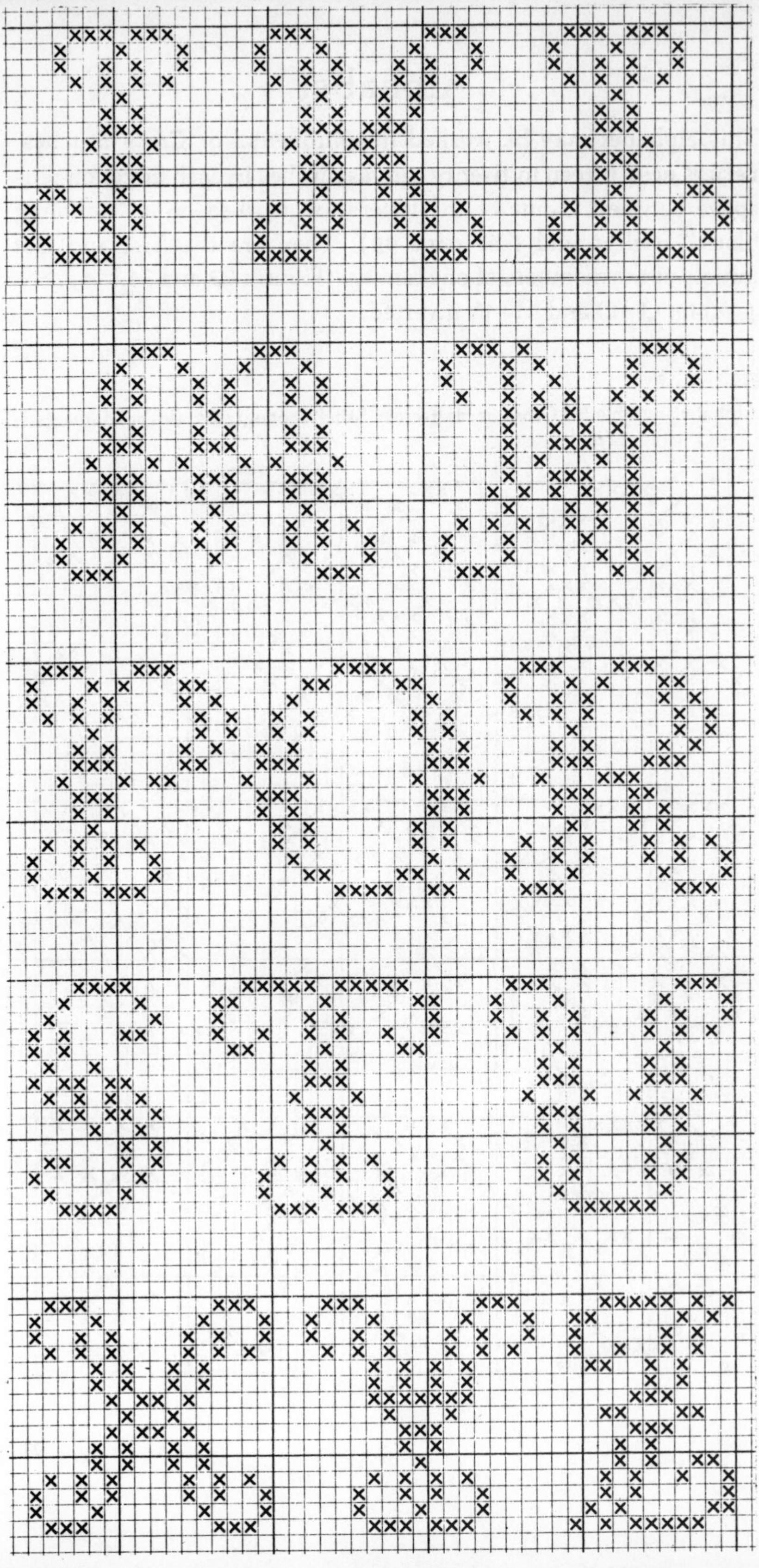

Tumbling Blocks

This is a familiar pattern seen in antique quilts and old marquetry (inlaid wood). The optical illusion is achieved by shading three geometric shapes in a specific manner.

Of the three geometric shapes, one is square or rectangular, and the other two are rhomboid. (Figures 75 and 76.) Traditionally, the squares are light, and the rhomboids alternate medium and dark. The medium and dark shades may change colors in alternate rows.

Tumbling blocks are handsome on large wall hangings worked in rug yarns or on handbags or book covers worked in very small gauge.

The large pattern is shown in graph outline in Figure 75. Practice this pattern until you understand its construction. Then create a framework of several rows of rhomboids in two neutral shades, and fill the white centers with a patchwork of stitch patterns.

A variation of the tumbling blocks pattern is established with a series of rectangles (Figures 77, A and 78, A) or squares (Figures 77, B and 78, B) worked in a diagonal line with corners touching. Place either one of the rhomboid shapes adjacent to the squares or rectangles, and then repeat the first row. Watch the optical illusion take shape.

You can change the length and width of one shape and adjust the other two, but be consistent with color placement.

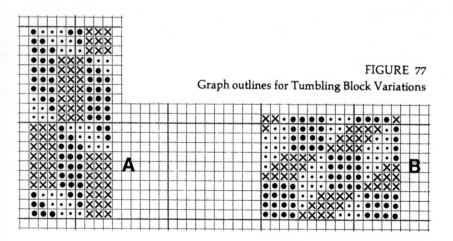

FIGURE 77
Graph outlines for Tumbling Block Variations

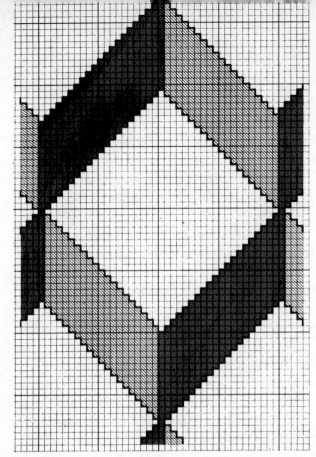

FIGURE 75 Graph outline unit for Tumbling Blocks

FIGURE 78 Tumbling Block Variations

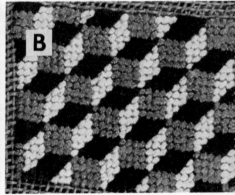

FIGURE 7
Tumbling Blocks

76

Small Interwoven Patterns

These patterns look best when outlined in dark cross stitches. Fill in Basketweave Stitch in one or two colors, or create ribbons of random widths and fill with a variety of stitch patterns. The center squares indicate the background behind the ribbons. They are left open here so that the interwoven strips may be seen more clearly, but they should be filled in. (Figures 79 and 80.)

FIGURE 79 Graph outlines for Woven Ribbons

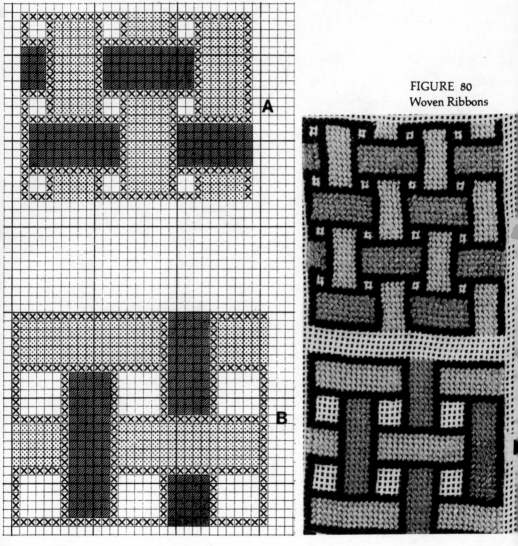

FIGURE 80
Woven Ribbons

Houndstooth Pattern

This is a classic pattern used in weaving. It is assembled with four rectangles drawn in four directions and converging at a center point. (Figures 81 and 82.)

The patterns resemble pinwheels, and they alternate colors in a diagonal line across the fabric. Study Figures 81 and 82 and work a sample in two colors.

This is an excellent repeat pattern that looks as well in petit point on a small billfold cover as it does in quick point on an area rug.

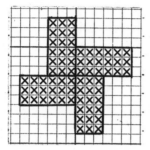

FIGURE 81
Graph outline for Houndstooth

FIGURE 82
Houndstooth

Gingham

One of the most familiar checked patterns, gingham is easy to duplicate in needlepoint. It consists of one basic square shape. The gingham effect is achieved through the precise placement of color.

Traditionally, gingham colors are white plus two shades of any given color. On a scale of one to five, one being the darkest, the two shades used are two and five.

One row alternates white and light shade squares and the next row alternates the light and dark shades. Study the gingham pattern in Figure 83 and work up a small sample. No graph is needed. This pattern can be worked in petit point as well as in large Cross Stitch. The background on the lady bug tricycle seat cover (color page C2) is blue gingham.

FIGURE 83
Gingham Pattern in Continental or Basketweave Stitch

Woven Ribbons

This is a small all-purpose pattern that may be enlarged or reduced by adjusting the width of the ribbons. The outline of the ribbons is worked in Cross Stitch on a diagonal line like the Basketweave. (See Basketweave Stitch detail in Figure 10.)

The ribbons are filled in with Basketweave, using one or two colors. The centers at the crossover point are left open, creating a small white cross in canvas threads. (Figures 84 and 85.) The handbag on color page C1 uses the woven ribbon pattern.

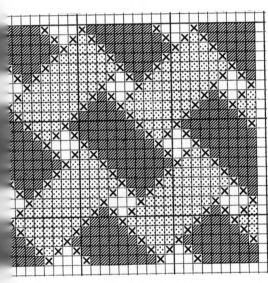

FIGURE 84
Graph outline for Diagonal Woven Ribbons with unworked centers (see color page C1, Bottom, C).

FIGURE 85
Diagonal Woven Ribbons

Borders and Small Patterns

Borders and small patterns have many uses, and anyone interested in needlework should have a collection of them. Because the pattern units are fairly small, they provide an excellent practice opportunity for beginners. They should always be worked in counted stitches.

Graphs and photographs are provided for all the borders. (Figures 86, 87, and 88.) Each border is a series of small patterns that may be used individually in miniature needlepoint or in multiple widths for wider borders. Work in two or three compatible colors.

Borders that square a piece of needlework should be worked in Cross Stitch or Basketweave to assure straight lines and sharp corners. Tent Stitches may distort the canvas, and this will often show even after careful blocking.

The tiny butterfly repeat patterns in Figure 89 may be worked in one or more colors in miniature needlepoint. Count stitches in Tent or Cross Stitch.

FIGURE 89
Butterfly Repeat Patterns

FIGURE 88
Graph outline for Butterfly Repeat Patterns

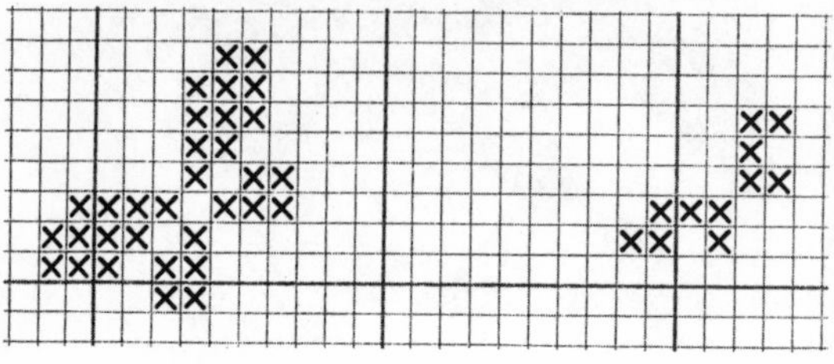

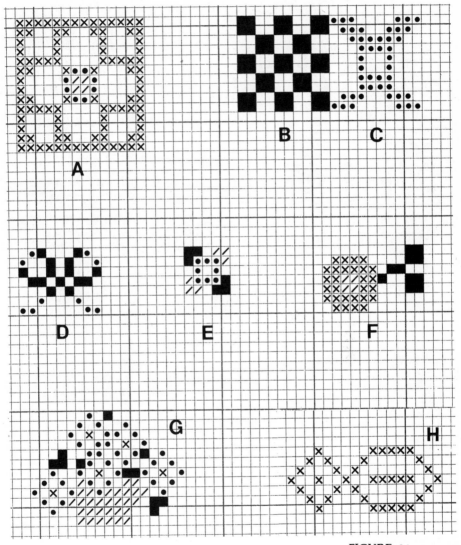

FIGURE 86
Graph outline for Cross Stitch Borders

Purses

(See color page C2.)

These two small purses (Figures 90 and 91) are available in kits from Toni Totes (see List of Suppliers on pages 127-128). The graph outline may also be adapted to small pillows. See general directions for enlarging and tracing design on canvas (page 11).

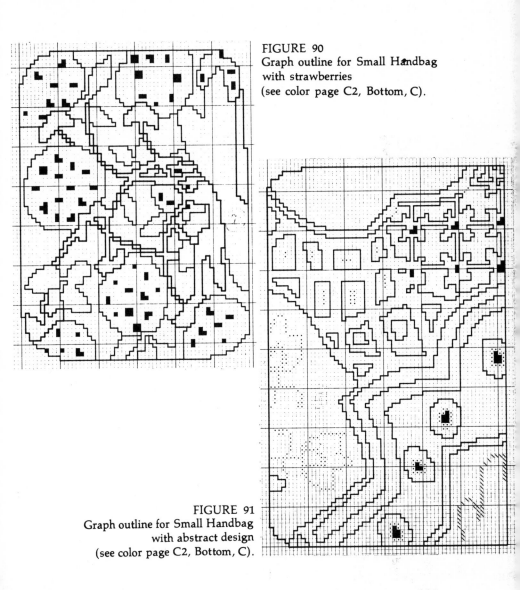

FIGURE 90
Graph outline for Small Handbag
with strawberries
(see color page C2, Bottom, C).

FIGURE 91
Graph outline for Small Handbag
with abstract design
(see color page C2, Bottom, C).

FIGURE 87
Cross Stitch Borders

Lacy Window Hanging

The even weave of needlepoint canvas is attractive enough to be incorporated into a design instead of being covered as a background.

Figure 92 shows a Cross Stitch pattern worked on # 4 double-thread canvas. The off-white yarn matches the canvas. Work with two-ply Persian-type yarn. Place the Cross Stitches as indicated in the stitch detail insert in Figure 92A.

Begin at the center fold, and count each stitch as one Cross Stitch. Over-all dimensions are 20" × 24", including border. To hang on a window, stitch a strip of commercial binding under the seams to keep them straight. Fold and stitch the top and bottom like a curtain and slip onto two curtain rods.

Figures 93 and 94 show the needlework in daytime and nighttime.

FIGURE 92A

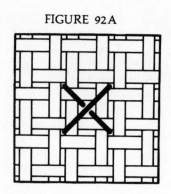

FIGURE 92
Graph outline for open-work
window hanging in Cross Stitch

FIGURE 93
Window Hanging, daytime view

FIGURE 94 Window Hanging, nighttime view

Beaver

(See color page C3.)

This is a very good beginner project and an exercise in Tent Stitch shapes. The flowers, hands and feet, and blades of grass are all simple shapes that may be used to translate other "coloring book" drawings such as this one. The link chain border may also be adapted to other designs. (Figure 95.)

FIGURE 95

Graph outline for Beaver ◢ and 1 = Dark green (see color page C3, Top, B) ⊡ and 2 = Light green; ☒ and 3 = Blue; ▣ and 4 = Red; ◩ and 5 = Yellow; 6 = Orange; 7 = White; 8 = Pink.

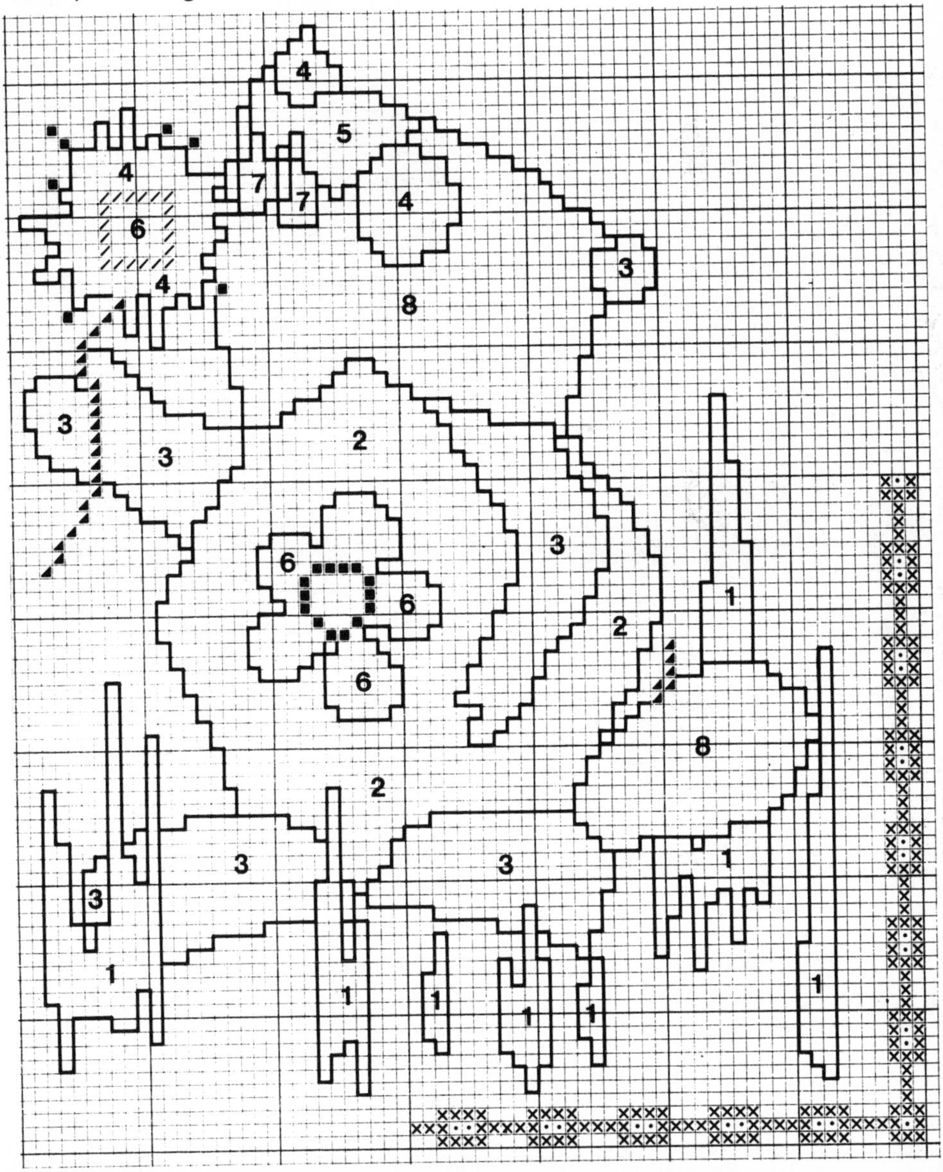

Tennis Racquet Cover
with Sneakers

(See color page C1.)

Canvas # 10 or # 12 will fit on a blank Toni Totes racquet cover
(see List of Suppliers on pages 127-128). Sneakers are worked in
shades of blue-green, charcoal, and cream on a red background.
Use the counted stitch method, or enlarge and outline on canvas.
(Figure 96.)

FIGURE 96 Diagram for Tennis Racquet Cover with Sneakers
(see color page C1, Bottom, A).

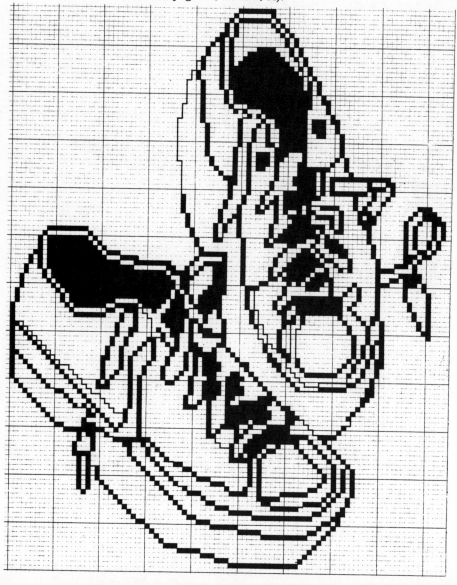

Doll Pillow

(See color page C3.)

To make this pillow, use the counted-stitch method, or enlarge and outline on canvas. This pattern may be enlarged on # 5 or # 4 canvas and finished as a small rug with a simple background. (Figure 97.)

To finish doll, block and place face-down on a square of velveteen. Machine stitch all around on the needlepoint side, leaving an opening at the bottom. Cut out shape of doll, leaving a ¹/₂″ margin. Clip into corners around the neck to facilitate stuffing. Turn right-side out and stuff firmly with dacron polyester or nylon stockings. Hand stitch bottom opening closed.

FIGURE 97

Graph for Doll Pillow (see color page C3, Top, C) ☒ = Violet; ■ = Black; ⊡ and 1 = Red; 2 = Green.

Bokara Design

(See color page C1.)

This adaptation from an antique rug is worked in Cross Stitch on # 10 double-mesh canvas. The colors are rust-red, turquoise, gold, cream, and navy. This is a very good design for a pillow, footstool, or (enlarged on # 4 canvas) small rug.

Add as many pattern units as necessary to increase the size of the project, but remember to adjust the border so that it fits properly around the design. This is best accomplished on graph paper. Geometric units are very flexible and may be easily altered by adding or removing one stitch or by adjusting the space between stitches. (Figure 98.)

FIGURE 98

Graph for Bokara Design (see color page C1, Bottom, B)   ☒ and 1 = Rust red; ◪ and 2 = Turquoise;   ▣ and 3 = Cream;   ⊞ and 4 = Gold;   ■ = Navy.

Two-color Floral Design

(See color page C1.)

This is an old fashioned two-color design. It is worked in the Cashmere Stitch pattern. Check general instructions for counting stitches and for the Cashmere Stitch pattern, and place one stitch unit for each counted square. Use # 10 single-mesh canvas.

If the Tent Stitch is used instead of the Cashmere, allow four stitches for each counted square (two down and two across), or use # 5 canvas to enlarge the gauge. (Figure 99.)

FIGURE 99

Diagram outline for Red and White Floral Design worked in Mosaic Stitch Pattern (see color page C1, Bottom, D).

Eagle

(See color page C2.)

The eagle is an Alice Peterson painted canvas with a blank background available in most stores. Figure 100 shows a graph outline for those with artistic ability and on pages 117-119 are instructions for creating a shaded background. Dimensions are 18″ × 18″.

The colors in the background are Paternayan Persian: 723, 731, 733, 741, and 743 (see List of Suppliers).

FIGURE 100 Graph outline for Eagle (see color page C2, Top, A)

Leopards

(See color page C4.)

These gorgeous leopard heads (Figure 101) are worked on # 10 canvas (mono white). The actual dimensions are 18″ × 24″.

Yarns: full three-ply Paternayan translated from graph as follows:
Black = Black
Dark Gray = # 134
Dapple = # 136
Fine Dots = # 166
Bold dots = # 280
White = # 020 or 012
Eyes = Light gold and dark gold
Cross = # 440
Half-cross = # 441
Dots = # 005
Trellis background = # 526

The symbols indicate shading, and the numbers indicate yarn colors. The trellis pattern is shown in Figure 103, E.

Work black outlines and eyes first. Finish the leopards according to general instructions on pages 120-125. Instructions for trellis background are on pages 117-119.

FIGURE 101 Graph outline for Leopards (see front cover). Diagram (insert).

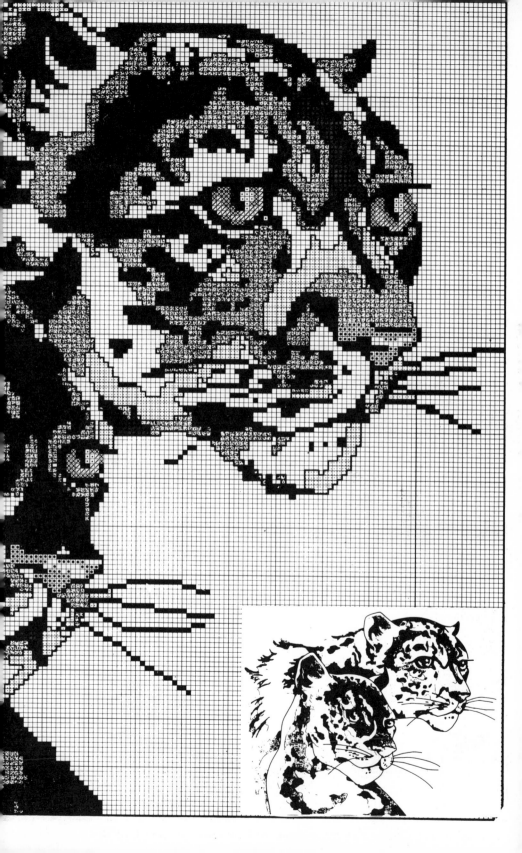

Poppies

(See color page C1.)

MATERIALS: 20″ × 20″ mono canvas # 12
1 ounce each deep purple, dark red or magenta, medium purple, light green, and white
2 ounces each light magenta, light purple, and black

Enlarge design according to general instructions, leaving a 1″ margin on each side. Go over the outlines with a medium-point felt pen, rounding them off. Tape enlargement to a flat surface, and place the canvas over it. Fasten in a few places with push pins and trace outline with a fine-point felt acrylic marking pen. Color in areas lightly, and work in Basketweave Stitch. (Figure 102.)

FIGURE 102
Diagram outline for Poppies (see color page C1, Top, D) Black = Black; 1 = White; 2 = Light magenta; 3 = Dark magenta; 4 = Wine color; 5 = Medium purple; 6 = Lavender; 7 = Moss green; 8 = Dark purple.

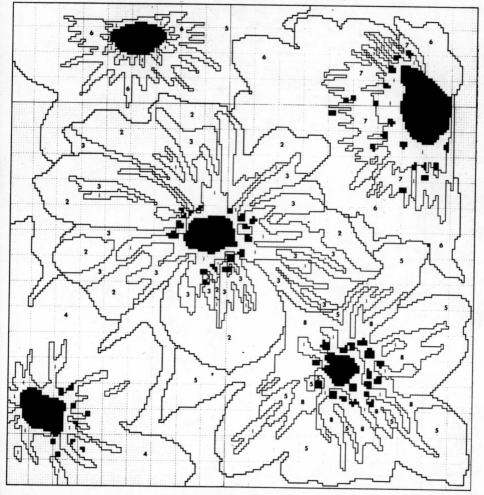

Background Stitches: Flat, Trellis, and Shaded

Traditionally, needlepoint canvas is covered completely with stitches. After the central design is finished, the background must be worked with the same care and accuracy.

Background yarn should be selected along with the rest of the yarns, and it is a good idea to assemble the colors on a skein of background color rather than on the canvas.

Background stitches should also be chosen carefully. Too much texture may overwhelm a delicate design or distract from one that is very striking.

A flat, one-color background is often the safest if not the most exciting choice. Add more interest by threading two closely related shades in the same family of color. From time to time work in one shade only. This creates a slightly mottled effect that resembles hand-dyed yarns.

Another alternative is the open trellis. Here, the canvas threads are incorporated into the pattern, and the effect is light and airy. The needlework on the cover of this book has a green trellis background.

The stitch technique for the open trellis is like Tent Stitch. Work it in continuous horizontal rows, skipping a stitch or two at regular intervals. The yarn is carried under the exposed canvas so that any lining or backing will not show through.

There are six trellis patterns with enlarged details shown in Figures 103 and 104 (the background on the cover is "E"). They are very small repeats and should be worked one row at a time. The trellis requires about the same amount of yarn as the Tent Stitch, but the work is not as distortive.

Backgrounds may be shaded, blended, or worked in small patterns such as Gingham or a two-tone Houndstooth. The simplest way to shade is to work with two closely related hues in the same color family. Work the hues singly or together, alternating casually. The over-all effect will resemble hand-dyed yarns.

Blending is not a beginner's project. It takes a great deal of practice plus a better than average eye for color. It cannot be explained in step-by-step instructions.

FIGURE 104 Enlarged details for Trellis Stitch Patterns

The eagle landing on a tree branch with the sky and water in the background (see color page C2) illustrates one method of blending background colors. It is worked in five shades of Persian yarn worked in a stagger system as follows:

Two-ply A
One-ply each A and B
Two-ply B
One-ply each B and C
Two-ply C
One-ply each C and C
Two-ply D
One-ply each D and E
Two-ply E

The same system may be adapted to three-ply yarn on a # 10 mesh. Simply remove one ply from one strand and replace it with a ply from the next shade. It is a challenging project and well worth the effort. Beginners should start with two or three shades and branch out slowly into a more ambitious project.

FIGURE 103
Trellis Stitch Patterns for Background

XX

FINISHING AND MOUNTING NEEDLEWORK

Blocking Needlework

Blocking is the method by which needlework is straightened and stitches evened. Blocking is a finishing process and always necessary unless the needlework was stitched on a frame.

Crewel and Bargello stitchery fluff out beautifully with blocking, and a good blocking can do wonders for any distorted canvas.

The best blocking surface is composition board. This is a specially processed material available in lumber yards. It does not warp, and it accommodates nails without splitting or throwing off splinters.

Buy a composition board that is a few inches larger than the largest work you are likely to block. For any project larger than 30″ × 30″, I recommend professional blocking.

You will also need a box of heavy-duty inch-long nails with large heads, a good heavy hammer, a thick terry towel, an iron, a pencil, and a ruler.

With pencil and ruler, outline the original outer dimensions of the entire canvas. Draw lines right on the board, and place the work to be blocked within this outline. Of the four corners in the canvas, two will be very pointed (Figure 105, BB) and the other two rather shallow (Figure 105, AA). The last two (opposite corners) should be nailed first. Fasten one into the outlined corner with two or three nails; pull the other one in the opposite direction and nail it into that corner. These two corners will offer the most resistance to blocking, so be sure to fasten them securely with several nails. Now pull the lateral sides of the canvas and nail them along the penciled outline. Drive nails halfway into the board about 1″ apart.

FIGURE 105

FIGURE 106

Blunt-nosed pliers are helpful in stretching canvas, and nails should be driven into the unfinished margins only.

A distorted canvas should be·blocked face-up so that the stitches can be watched as they are being stretched into shape. The crucial test is the stretch point between the A corners in Figure 106. The better it squares off, the more even the needlework will be.

When blocking is completed, place a damp (not wet) terry towel over the canvas and glide a hot iron over it until it stops steaming. Repeat this several times. Let dry at least twenty-four hours, and and then steam again. Remove nails after two or three days, and let the canvas rest a day or two. If some of the distortion reappears, there is little you can do. No additional blocking will restore the canvas.

Framing or upholstering will preserve the design, but a soft hanging or a pillow will have to be adjusted by cutting away the distorted corners.

Beginners should avoid geometric borders worked with slanted stitches. See the section on distortion in stitchery on pages 79-83.

Note: It is not necessary to soak canvas needlework before blocking. Soaking makes the work slippery; and if too much sizing penetrates the yarn, the stitches will stiffen as they dry. If canvas resists stretching, mist it slightly to relax the threads. Use a misting device designed for spraying house plants. Raised or textured stitches should not be pressed at all. Mist the canvas on the reverse side, and block it right-side up.

Framing Needlework

Needlework cannot be framed like a photograph or poster, nor should it be glued to a board. For best results, it must be stretched on a frame.

The best frame for needlework is the simple, sturdy artist's frame. These frames are sold in individual strips of 6" and up. Each end of the strip is grooved and mitered for easy assembly.

After a needlework is stretched on an artist's frame, it can be slipped into a decorative frame. These come in packages of prefinished strips of one length. Since frame sizes are somewhat limited, check the supply of ready-made frames in your area before choosing the design and dimensions of your needlework.

Once the frames are selected, finish and block the needlepoint. Assemble the artist's frame, steam the needlepoint to relax canvas (see blocking information), and place it over the frame. The worked area should not extend over the edge of the frame.

Place a few push pins into the corners and around the sides to keep the canvas from shifting. Fold the unworked margin of canvas over the edge of the frame, and staple the center point on each side of the frame. The rows of stitches should look straight and the needlework smooth and even without overstretching.

Staple all around the frame, folding corners neatly as shown in Figure 107. If the staples protrude slightly, hammer them in. If a professional stapler is not available, use carpet tacks placed $1/2''$ apart.

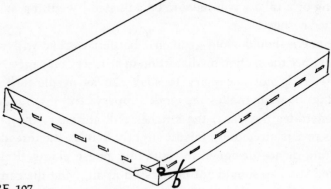

FIGURE 107
Stretching needlework on artist's frame

Cut the canvas along the edges, and insert finished piece into a decorative frame. Do not place glass over the needlework unless you are framing a fragile antique; and in that case, have a professional do the job.

Note: The edge of the decorative frame should cover one or two rows of stitched canvas all around. Allow for this in the preliminary planning of the needlepoint. Antique frames can be used for needlework if they are deep enough to accommodate an artist's frame. A frame that was used for an oil painting is more suitable than one used for a photograph. Custom frames should always be handled by a professional.

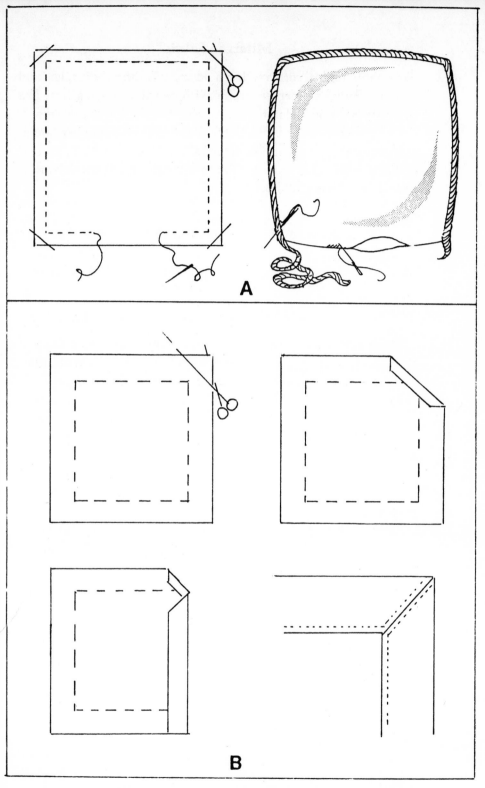

FIGURE 108 How to make a pillow and how to miter fabric

Mitering Fabric

For neatly folded corners, learn to miter fabric rectangles and squares. Indicate a center outline with pencil or basting line. If a design is embroidered in the center, this can serve as the outline.

Clip the corners and fold to the inner outline. Fold over lateral sides until they meet on the diagonal miter line. Baste all around and sew with small stitches. Remove bastings and press work if necessary. (Figure 108, B.)

How to Make a Needlepoint Pillow

MATERIALS: Fabric backing (velvet, upholstery fabric, duck, linen, etc.) the size of needlepoint plus 1" margin
Decorative cording
Pillow filler (dacron polyester or down and feathers)

Block and square needlepoint. Press fabric and place the two right sides together. Baste all around to keep pieces from shifting, and cut away any canvas that extends over the fabric margin.

Machine stitch as indicated in Figure 108, A. Stitch two rows at the widest setting *into* the top row of the needlework. Clip corners and cut edges all around to $1/2"$. Turn case right-side out, poke out corners with your fingers, and slip in the pillow filler.

The opening will fold in automatically and should be sewed closed with small stitches. (These can be removed and later replaced for cleaning or repair.)

Decorative cording is optional. Sew it along the edge with small stitches and matching thread. Tuck the ends skillfully into the opening before stitching.

XXX

LIST OF SUPPLIERS

Retail Only

La Stitcherie
72 Middle Neck Road
Great Neck, New York 11021

Canvas, yarn, kits, custom designs

Wholesale and Retail

Toni Toes of Vermont, Inc.
Route 100
South Londonderry, Vermont 05155

Handbags, kits for tennis racquet covers, belts for needlepoint, plastic enclosures
Will send catalogue

Walbead, Inc.
38 West 37th Street
New York, New York 10018

Beads, sequins, macrame
Will send catalogue

Wholesale Only

Paternayan Brothers, Inc.
312 East 95th Street
New York, New York 10028

Paternayan Persian yarn, canvas and needles, rug and crewel yarns, Rya cloth

Craft Yarns of Rhode Island
P.O. Box 151
Harrisville, R.I.

Three-ply Persian-type yarn, quick-point yarn, needlepoint canvas

Coats and Clark's
P.O. Box 1966
Stamford, Connecticut 06904

Cotton and rayon embroidery threads and rug yarns, craft yarns (acrylic washable), acrylic Persian-type yarn, needles

Handwork Tapestries
114 B Allen Blvd.
Farmingdale, New York 11735

Persian-type yarn, Laine Colbert three-ply tapestry yarn, Colbert six, French silk, canvas

Art Needlework Treasure Trove P.O. Box 2440 Grand Central Station New York, New York 10017	Canvas, yarns, linens, embroidery fabrics, and supplies
Howard Needlework Supply Co., Inc. 919 Third Avenue New York, New York 10022	Canvas and embroidery fabric in linen, cotton, and polyester
William E. Wright Co. One Penn Plaza New York, New York 10001	Lace
E.T. Group Ltd. 230 Fifth Avenue New York, New York 10017	Paternayan yarns, Alice Peterson painted canvases, Rya cloth
George Wells The Ruggery Cedar Swamp Road Glen Head, New York 11545	Rug yarns, linen and Rya cloth, undyed yarn, special dyes for wool yarns, Hectograph pencils
Astor Place Ltd. 260 Main Avenue Stirling, New Jersey 07980	Painted canvases and packaged kits
Cute and Custom 1A Munson Court Melville, New York 11746	Painted canvases and packaged kits
Needlepoint U.S.A. 37 West 57th Street New York, New York 10019	Painted canvases and packaged kits

Note: For all inquiries to dealers, enclose a self-addressed stamped envelope.

then we can use this to connect $y_l(n)$ and $y_k(n)$. Once we have relations which are true for all $n \geq 0$, with all variables in the form $y_i(n)$,
we can simplify by replacing each $y_i(n)$ by y_i, obtaining an invariant which may still contain occurrences of $y_i(0)$.

Whenever possible, known information from the entry invariant
$p(\bar{x}, \bar{y})$ may be used to obtain $\bar{y}(0)$. When the variables are initialized
immediately before entering the loop, $p(\bar{x}, \bar{y})$ will indicate the exact
values of $\bar{y}(0)$. However, even when this is not the case, $p(\bar{x}, \bar{y})$ may
often contain valuable information about $\bar{y}(0)$.

It is important to note that any predicate obtained as above,
say from (a') or (b'), is not simply a candidate for an invariant, *but
is actually an invariant*. This is because substituting the correct initial
value in place of $\bar{y}(0)$ ensures that the relation obtained is true the
first time the cutpoint is reached, and the use of $r_\alpha(\bar{x}, \bar{y})$ in obtaining
the recurrence equations ensures that the relation is true at sub-
sequent times the cutpoint is reached.

Recall that the transformation from the recurrence equation (2.1)
to (2.2) was made under the assumption that there was a single path
around the loop as in Figure 2.3. The above discussion can easily
be extended to the case of a loop with several possible paths—by
using **if-then-else** expressions. For example, considering the loop of
Figure 2.4, with two paths around the loop, Equation (2.1) expands
to two equations:

$$\sim t_1(\bar{x}, \bar{y}(n-1)) \wedge t_2(\bar{x}, \bar{y}(n-1)) \supset \bar{y}(n) = f_1(\bar{x}, \bar{y}(n-1)),$$

and

$$\sim t_1(\bar{x}, \bar{y}(n-1)) \wedge \sim t_2(\bar{x}, \bar{y}(n-1)) \supset \bar{y}(n) = f_2(\bar{x}, \bar{y}(n-1)).$$

These can be combined into one statement, as

$$\sim t_1(\bar{x}, \bar{y}(n-1)) \supset [\text{if } t_2(\bar{x}, \bar{y}(n-1))$$
$$\text{then } \bar{y}(n) = f_1(\bar{x}, \bar{y}(n-1))$$
$$\text{else } \bar{y}(n) = f_2(\bar{x}, \bar{y}(n-1))].$$

Since $t_1(\bar{x}, \bar{y})$ controls the exit from the block, and does not
affect the choice between the two paths around the loop, it can
be ignored, as before, giving the stronger condition

$$\text{if } t_2(\bar{x}, \bar{y}(n-1)) \text{ then } \bar{y}(n) = f_1(\bar{x}, \bar{y}(n-1))$$
$$\text{else } \bar{y}(n) = f_2(\bar{x}, \bar{y}(n-1)). \qquad (2.3)$$

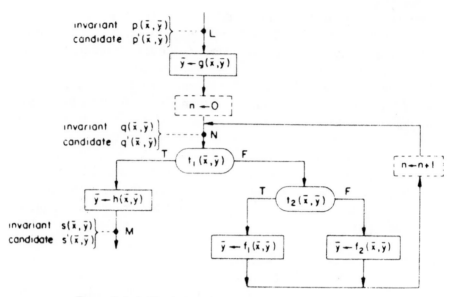

Figure 2.4. A Block Containing a Loop with Two Paths.

Equations of this form can then be put in iterative form, and treated just like equations of form (2.2).

3.2. Generating invariants from tests

So far we have concentrated on generating invariants from assignment statements, and the tests did not play a major role. Now we will show how the tests can aid in extracting additional invariants from the loop.

Suppose the block has the paths $\alpha_1, \alpha_2, ..., \alpha_k$ $(k \geqslant 1)$ from the cutpoint N around the loop back to N. Again we shall use an obvious fact: whenever N is reached during execution, either the block has just been entered, or control was previously at N and one of the paths $\alpha_1, ..., \alpha_k$ was followed. Letting n be the counter of the block, this can be written more precisely as

$$n = 0 \ \lor \ [R_{\alpha_1}(\bar{x}, \bar{y}(n-1)) \lor R_{\alpha_2}(\bar{x}, \bar{y}(n-1)) \lor \cdots$$
$$\lor R_{\alpha_k}(\bar{x}, \bar{y}(n-1))]. \tag{2.4}$$

This claim is clearly always true at N. By expressing $\bar{y}(n-1)$

in terms of $\bar{y}(n)$—using the recurrence equations given by (2.1)—and adding known information about $\bar{y}(0)$, we can often simplify (2.4). Again, if we obtain relations which are true for all $n \geq 0$, and all variables are expressed as $y_i(n)$, we can remove the parameter n to obtain an invariant.

We demonstrate some of the above techniques on a program. Note that we do not claim that this program is correct.

Example A. Program[2] A of Figure 2.5 is intended to divide x_1 by x_2 within tolerance x_3, where x_1, x_2, and x_3 are real numbers satisfying $0 \leq x_1 < x_2$ and $0 < x_3$; the final value of y_4 is supposed to satisfy $x_1/x_2 - x_3 < y_4 \leq x_1/x_2$ at the haltpoint H. For clarity we have explicitly added the counter n to the program. There are two paths from the cutpoint N around the loop and back to N: the right path following the T-branch from the test $x_1 < y_1 + y_2$, and the left path following the corresponding F-branch. By using (2.1) we have for each path:

Right path:

$$[y_3(n-1){>}x_3 \wedge x_1 < y_1(n-1)+y_2(n-1)]$$
$$\supset [y_1(n){=}y_1(n-1) \wedge$$
$$y_2(n){=}y_2(n-1)/2 \wedge$$
$$y_3(n){=}y_3(n-1)/2 \wedge$$
$$y_4(n){=}y_4(n-1)].$$

Left path:

$$[y_3(n-1){>}x_3 \wedge x_1 {\geq} y_1(n-1)+y_2(n-1)]$$
$$\supset [y_1(n) = y_1(n-1) + y_2(n-1) \wedge$$
$$y_2(n) = y_2(n-1)/2 \wedge$$
$$y_3(n) = y_3(n-1)/2 \wedge$$
$$y_4(n) = y_4(n-1) + y_3(n-1)/2].$$

---

[2] This program is based on Wensley's (1958) division algorithm. Note that we use a vector assignment notation, where, for example, $(y_1, y_4) \leftarrow (y_1 + y_2, y_4 + y_3/2)$ means that $y_1 \leftarrow y_1 + y_2$ and $y_4 \leftarrow y_4 + y_3/2$ simultaneously.

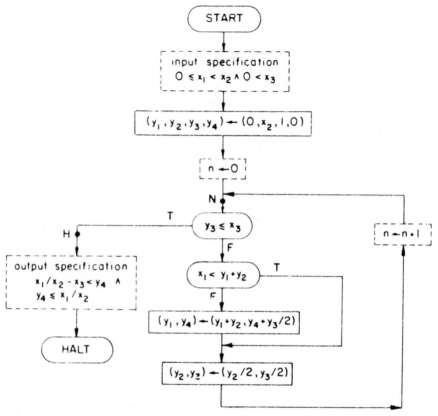

Figure 2.5. Program A. Real Division within Tolerance.

Since the assignments to y_2 and y_3 are not affected by which path is used, we may ignore the path conditions, obtaining

$$y_2(n) = y_2(n-1)/2 \ \wedge \ y_3(n) = y_3(n-1)/2.$$

Both of these are in the iterative form (b) and may be solved to yield

$$y_2(n) = y_2(0) \cdot \prod_{i=1}^{n} \frac{1}{2} \ \wedge \ y_3(n) = y_3(0) \cdot \prod_{i=1}^{n} \frac{1}{2}.$$

Since it is clear that $y_2(0) = x_2$ and $y_3(0) = 1$ at N and that $\prod_{i=1}^{n} 1/2 = 1/2^n$, we have (dropping the parameter n) the invariants

(A1) $y_2 = x_2/2^n$ at N,

and

(A2) $y_3 = 1/2^n$ at N.

These may be combined to yield the additional invariant

(A3) $y_2 = x_2 \cdot y_3$ at N.

For variables y_1 and y_4, we apply the techniques used to obtain Equation (2.3): Ignoring the exit test $y_3 \leqslant x_3$ and expressing the effect of the branching by using **if-then-else**, the resulting recurrence relations are

$$y_1(n) = \text{if } x_1 < y_1(n-1) + y_2(n-1)$$
$$\text{then } y_1(n-1)$$
$$\text{else } y_1(n-1) + y_2(n-1),$$

and

$$y_4(n) = \text{if } x_1 < y_1(n-1) + y_2(n-1)$$
$$\text{then } y_4(n-1)$$
$$\text{else } y_4(n-1) + y_3(n-1)/2.$$

Both of these are in iterative form, and we can obtain the summations

$$y_1(n) = y_1(0) + \sum_{i=1}^{n} [\text{if } x_1 < y_1(i-1) + y_2(i-1)$$
$$\text{then } 0$$
$$\text{else } y_2(i-1)]$$

$$y_4(n) = y_4(0) + \sum_{i=1}^{n} [\text{if } x_1 < y_1(i-1) + y_2(i-1)$$
$$\text{then } 0$$
$$\text{else } y_3(i-1)/2].$$

We will use the invariant (A3), that $y_2 = x_2 \cdot y_3$ at N, in order to bring the two summations to an identical form. Substituting $x_2 \cdot y_3(i-1)$ for $y_2(i-1)$ in the else part of the equation for $y_1(n)$, factoring out x_2, and dividing by 2 inside the summation and multiplying by 2 outside, we obtain

$$y_1(n) = y_1(0) + 2x_2 \cdot \sum_{i=1}^{n} [\text{if } x_1 < y_1(i-1) + y_2(i-1)$$
$$\text{then } 0$$
$$\text{else } y_3(i-1)/2].$$

We have expressed $y_1(n)$ and $y_4(n)$ in terms of the same summation, which thus can be used to connect these two variables. Substituting $y_1(0) = 0$ and $y_4(0) = 0$, we obtain

$$y_1(n) = 2x_2 \cdot \sum_{i=1}^{n} [\text{if } x_1 < y_1(i-1) + y_2(i-1)\\ \text{then } 0 \\ \text{else } y_3(i-1)/2]$$
$$= 2x_2 \cdot y_4(n).$$

Thus we have the invariant

(A4) $y_1 = 2x_2 \cdot y_4$ at N.

We now turn to Equation (2.4), using the tests of the loop to generate additional invariants. We have the fact

$n = 0$

$\lor [y_3(n-1) > x_3 \land x_1 < y_1(n-1) + y_2(n-1)]$ (right path)

$\lor [y_3(n-1) > x_3 \land x_1 \geqslant y_1(n-1) + y_2(n-1)]$ (left path).

For each path, we now use the equations for $\bar{y}(n)$ obtained from (2.1) to express $\bar{y}(n-1)$ in terms of $\bar{y}(n)$. For the right path we will use the fact that $y_1(n) = y_1(n-1)$, $y_2(n) = y_2(n-1)/2$, and $y_3(n) = y_3(n-1)/2$, while for the left path we will use the fact that $y_1(n) = y_1(n-1) + y_2(n-1)$ and $y_3(n) = y_3(n-1)/2$. These substitutions will yield.

$n = 0$

$\lor [2y_3(n) > x_3 \land x_1 < y_1(n) + 2y_2(n)]$ (right path)

$\lor [2y_3(n) > x_3 \land x_1 \geqslant y_1(n)]$ (left path).

Removing the parametrization in terms of n, and separating the term involving y_3, we have the two new invariants at N,

$$[n = 0 \lor 2y_3 > x_3] \land [n = 0 \lor x_1 < y_1 + 2y_2 \lor x_1 \geqslant y_1].$$

To obtain stronger invariants, we can check whether the $n = 0$ case is subsumed in the other alternatives. The left conjunct may not be so reduced, and we have the invariant

(A5) $n = 0 \lor 2y_3 > x_3$ at N.

The $n = 0$ possibility in the right conjunct can easily be seen to be included in the other possibilities, since $y_1(0) = 0$ and $x_1 \geqslant 0$ imply that $x_1 \geqslant y_1(0)$. Thus we have the invariant

(A6) $x_1 < y_1 + 2y_2 \lor x_1 \geqslant y_1$ at N.

Note that invariant (A6) is a disjunction of the form $p \lor q$. This disjunction actually reflects the effect of taking the right path or the left path, respectively, around the loop. $\square$

4. Generation of Invariants: Heuristic Approach

We now describe several heuristic techniques which suggest promising candidate invariants. There is no guarantee that the candidates produced are actually invariants, and they must be checked (using Lemma A).

It is important to notice that when we are unable to establish that a candidate is an invariant, it should be saved to retry later. In the meantime, additional invariants or new candidates may have been developed that, along with the original candidate, satisfy Lemma A.

It should be clear that before an automatic system for generating invariants is practical, strong guidance must be provided for the application of the following rules, since, applied blindly, they could result in too many irrelevant candidates. Here we merely state some of the various possibilities in order to give the flavor of this approach.

4.1. Disjunct Elimination

Whenever we have established an invariant at a cutpoint i which is a disjunction of the form

$$p_1 \lor p_2 \lor \cdots \lor p_k \quad (k \geqslant 2),$$

we try to see whether any subdisjunction (in particular, each p_j alone) is itself an invariant at i. In the previous section, we actually used this approach when we eliminated the $n = 0$ alternative to obtain the invariant (A6).

4.2. Conjunct Elimination

Suppose we have at i a candidate which is a conjunction of the form

$$p_1 \wedge p_2 \wedge \cdots \wedge p_k \quad (k \geqslant 2),$$

and we have failed to prove that it is an invariant at i. One natural heuristic is to try a subconjunction (in particular, each p_j alone) as a "new" candidate. Note that the failure to prove $p_1 \wedge p_2 \wedge \cdots \wedge p_k$ an invariant says nothing about whether its subconjunctions are invariants. Theoretically, any nonempty subconjunction is a legitimate candidate and should be checked independently.

For the next three heuristics, we refer back to Figure 2.3.

4.3. Pushing Candidates Backward

Let us assume that $p(\bar{x}, \bar{y})$ is an established invariant at L and $q'(\bar{x}, \bar{y})$ is a candidate invariant at N. If the inductive step around the loop has been shown to establish $q'(\bar{x}, \bar{y})$ at N, then the only difficulty could be that $p(\bar{x}, \bar{y})$ did not imply $q'(\bar{x}, g(\bar{x}, \bar{y}))$. We then try

$$p'(\bar{x}, \bar{y}): \quad q'(\bar{x}, g(\bar{x}, \bar{y}))$$

as a new candidate at L. This will "fix" the problem with $q'(\bar{x}, \bar{y})$, but of course we must now prove $p'(\bar{x}, \bar{y})$ an invariant at L. Note that in any case $p'(\bar{x}, \bar{y})$ must be an invariant at L if we are to succeed in showing that $q'(\bar{x}, \bar{y})$ is an invariant at N and in this sense is the "weakest" possible precondition for the base case of the induction for $q'(\bar{x}, \bar{y})$.

A similar technique can also be used to generate candidates at N:

Let us assume that $q(\bar{x}, \bar{y})$ is an established invariant at N and $s'(\bar{x}, \bar{y})$ is a candidate invariant at M. Since $s'(\bar{x}, \bar{y})$ is reached only from N, the reason we were not able to prove it an invariant must be that $q(\bar{x}, \bar{y}) \wedge t(\bar{x}, \bar{y})$ could not be shown to imply $s'(\bar{x}, h(\bar{x}, \bar{y}))$. Thus we would like to find a candidate $q'(\bar{x}, \bar{y})$ at N such that

$$[q(\bar{x}, \bar{y}) \wedge q'(\bar{x}, \bar{y}) \wedge t(\bar{x}, \bar{y})] \supset s'(\bar{x}, h(\bar{x}, \bar{y})). \qquad (2.5)$$

Among the many possible choices of $q'(\bar{x}, \bar{y})$ which satisfy this condition are

$$q'(\bar{x}, \bar{y}): \quad t(\bar{x}, \bar{y}) \supset s'(\bar{x}, h(\bar{x}, \bar{y})),$$

or $\qquad q'(\overline{x}, \overline{y}): s'(\overline{x}, h(\overline{x}, \overline{y})).$

This first possibility is, just as above, the weakest possible assertion which satisfies (2.5), while the second is the strongest possible. A very useful third alternative to the above suggestions takes advantage of the transitivity of certain inequality or equality relations. For example, if we need a q' such that

$$q' \wedge B < C \supset A < C$$

where A, B, and C are any terms, then the relation $A \leqslant B$ is a natural candidate for q'.

Any candidate for $q'(\overline{x}, \overline{y})$ obtained from Equation (2.5) must be checked. Unfortunately, there are no clear-cut criteria for finding a $q'(\overline{x}, \overline{y})$ which will be easy to prove. If we fail to show some candidate $q'(\overline{x}, \overline{y})$ an invariant at N, some weaker version may nevertheless succeed. On the other hand, because of the "induction phenomenon", mentioned after Lemma A, it is quite possible that a stronger candidate $q'(\overline{x}, \overline{y})$ actually could be more easily proven.

4.4. Pushing Invariants Forward

Assuming that $p(\overline{x}, \overline{y})$ is an established invariant at L, a straightforward heuristic is to try to find a candidate $q'(\overline{x}, \overline{y})$ at N such that

$$p(\overline{x}, \overline{y}) \supset q'(\overline{x}, g(\overline{x}, \overline{y})).$$

The above equation ensures that the first time N is reached, $q'(\overline{x}, \overline{y})$ is true. Of course, in order to complete the proof that $q'(\overline{x}, \overline{y})$ is an invariant, the corresponding formula for the path around the loop must be considered.

Note that immediately after every assignment $y_i \leftarrow f(\overline{x}, \overline{y})$ where $f(\overline{x}, \overline{y})$ does not include y_i itself, we know that $y_i = f(\overline{x}, \overline{y})$ is an invariant. Also, after every text $t(\overline{x}, \overline{y})$ we can add the invariant $t(\overline{x}, \overline{y})$ on the T-branch, and $\sim t(\overline{x}, \overline{y})$ on the F-branch. Such invariants can also be pushed forward to generate useful candidates at the cutpoints.

4.5. Bounding Variables

One useful type of candidate for $q'(\overline{x}, y)$ at N is constructed by finding upper or lower bounds for the variables, expressed only in terms of *constant expressions* with respect to the block. That is, the bounds contain only constants, input variables, or other program variables which are unchanged inside the loop of the block.

Suppose that by considering $f(\bar{x}, \bar{y})$ and the invariant $q(\bar{x}, \bar{y})$ at N, we are able to identify a variable y_j which never decreases along the path around the loop. Now, if we can infer from $p(\bar{x}, \bar{y})$ an initial value $y_j(0) = E$ for y_j at N, where E is a constant expression with respect to the block, then we can conclude that $y_j \geqslant E$ is an invariant at N. Similarly, if y_j never increases, then $y_j \leqslant E$ is invariant.

A similar heuristic tries to establish that the variables maintain some data type, such as *integer* or *real,* during execution.

We will first illustrate the application of the heuristics in obtaining some additional invariants for the program of Example A, and then present a new example which will illustrate the possible interplay between the algorithmic and heuristic techniques.

Example A (continued). Let us consider again Program A of Figure 2.5. Applying the disjunct elimination rule of Section 4.1 to the invariant

(A6) $x_1 < y_1 + 2y_2 \lor x_1 \geqslant y_1$ at N,

we check first whether $x_1 < y_1 + 2y_2$ is itself an invariant. From Lemma A, we can show that

(a) $\forall \bar{x} [0 \leqslant x_1 < x_2 \land 0 < x_3 \supset x_1 < 0 + 2x_2]$ and

(b) $\forall \bar{x} \forall \bar{y} [x_1 < y_1 + 2y_2 \land y_3 > x_3 \land x_1 < y_1 + y_2$
$\supset x_1 < y_1 + y_2],$
$\forall \bar{x} \, \forall \bar{y} [x_1 < y_1 + 2y_2 \land y_3 > x_3 \land x_1 \geqslant y_1 + y_2$
$\supset x_1 < y_1 + y_2 + y_2].$

Since all of the conditions are true, we have the invariant

(A7) $x_1 < y_1 + 2y_2$ at N.

For $x_1 \geqslant y_1$, the second disjunct of (A6), we can show that

(a) $\forall \bar{x} [0 \leqslant x_1 < x_2 \land 0 < x_3 \supset x_1 \geqslant 0],$

(b) $\forall \bar{x} \, \forall \, \bar{y}[x_1 \geqslant y_1 \, \wedge \, y_3 > x_3 \, \wedge \, x_1 < y_1 + y_2 \supset x_1 \geqslant y_1]$,

$\forall \bar{x} \, \forall \, \bar{y}[x_1 \geqslant y_1 \, \wedge \, y_3 > x_3 \, \wedge \, x_1 \geqslant y_1 + y_2 \supset x_1 \geqslant y_1 + y_2]$.

Since these conditions are all true, we have shown that the second alternative is also an invariant, i.e.,

(A8) $x_1 \geqslant y_1$ at N.

We can combine the invariant (A4), $y_1 = 2x_2 \cdot y_4$, with (A8) and the input assertion $0 < x_2$ to obtain an upper bound on y_4 in terms of $\bar{x}$, i.e., the invariant

(A9) $y_4 \leqslant x_1/(2x_2)$ at N.

This invariant will be of special use later, in Sections 5 and 6, and in practice would be generated only when a need for such a bound arises.

Now, by pushing forward to H the invariants (A1) to (A9) at N, and adding the exit test $y_3 \leqslant x_3$, we obtain

(A10) $y_3 \leqslant x_3 \, \wedge \, y_2 = x_2/2^n \, \wedge \, y_3 = 1/2^n \, \wedge \, y_2 = x_2 \cdot y_3$

$\wedge \, y_1 = 2x_2 \cdot y_4 \, \wedge \, (n = 0 \, \vee \, 2y_3 > x_3) \, \wedge \, x_1 < y_1 + 2y_2$

$\wedge \, x_1 \geqslant y_1 \, \wedge \, y_4 \leqslant x_1/(2x_2)$ at H.   □

Example B. The program B shown in Figure 2.6 is supposed to perform integer division in a manner similar to computer hardware. For every integer input $x_1 \geqslant 0$ and $x_2 > 0$, we would like to have as output $y_1 = rem(x_1, x_2)$ and $y_4 = div(x_1, x_2)$, i.e., $x_1 = y_4 \cdot x_2 + y_1 \, \wedge \, 0 \leqslant y_1 < x_2 \, \wedge y_1, y_4 \in \{$integers$\}$. This program differs from the previous example in that it contains two loops, one after the other. The upper block, with counter n and cutpoint N, consists of a simple loop, while the lower block, with counter m and cutpoint M, consists of a loop with two paths. For convenience, we have added an additional cutpoint L between the blocks.

Our strategy will be to gather initially as many invariants as possible at N. The algorithmic techniques will be used to generate invariants at N directly, and then some of the heuristics presented above will be used to suggest additional invariants. We then push the invariants forward to cutpoint L, so that we have as many invariants as we

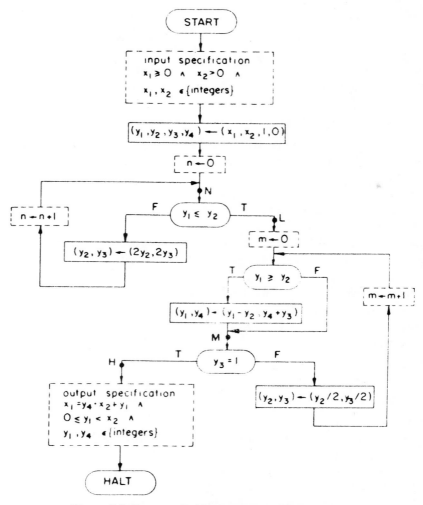

Figure 2.6. Program B. Hardware Integer Division.

can when the second block is first reached. Then we will employ the algorithmic techniques to generate invariants at M. Finally, we use heuristic techniques based on the invariants at L and M and the candidates implied by the output specification at H to generate additional invariants at M. We will not go into the problem of which heuristic rule to use first, but simply indicate how some candidates, which will indeed be useful invariants, can be found by using various heuristics.

Applying the algorithmic techniques for finding invariants at N, we obtain the equations

$$y_2(n) = y_2(0) \cdot \prod_{i=1}^{n} 2 = y_2(0) \cdot 2^n = x_2 \cdot 2^n \quad \text{at } N,$$

$$y_3(n) = y_3(0) \cdot \prod_{i=1}^{n} 2 = y_3(0) \cdot 2^n = 2^n \quad \text{at } N.$$

Thus we can obtain the invariants

(B1) $y_2 = x_2 \cdot 2^n \wedge y_3 = 2^n$ at N.

These can be combined to give

(B2) $y_2 = x_2 \cdot y_3$ at N.

By pushing forward the information in $\phi(\bar{x})$ and the initial asssignments (using the heuristic of Section 4.4), we get the additional invariants

(B3) $y_1 = x_1 \wedge y_4 = 0 \wedge y_1, y_2, y_3, y_4 \in \{\text{integers}\}$ at N.

Using the bounding variables rule of Section 4.5, we note that y_2 and y_3 are always increasing around the loop and, since $y_2(0) = x_2$ and $y_3(0) = 1$ at N, we obtain the invariants

(B4) $y_2 \geqslant x_2 \wedge y_3 \geqslant 1$ at N.

Note that (B4) could also be obtained directly from (B1) using the implicit invariant $n \geqslant 0$.

Using the T-branch of the test $y_1 \leqslant y_2$ and pushing forward to L the invariants at N, we have the invariants

(B5) $y_2 = x_2 \cdot 2^n \wedge y_3 = 2^n \wedge y_2 = x_2 \cdot y_3 \wedge y_1 = x_1 \wedge y_4 = 0 \wedge$

$y_1, y_2, y_3, y_4 \in \{\text{integers}\} \wedge y_2 \geqslant x_2 \wedge y_3 \geqslant 1 \wedge y_1 \leqslant y_2$ at L.

Generating invariants directly from the statements of the lower block, we first have the relations

$$y_2(m) = y_2(0)/2^m \quad \text{at } M,$$
$$y_3(m) = y_3(0)/2^m \quad \text{at } M.$$

Using the invariants $y_2 = x_2 \cdot 2^n$ and $y_3 = 2^n$ from (B5) to establish $y_2(0)$ and $y_3(0)$ at M, we obtain the invariants

(B6) $y_2 = x_2 \cdot 2^n/2^m \;\wedge\; y_3 = 2^n/2^m \;\wedge\; y_2 = x_2 \cdot y_3 \quad$ at M.

Using the same technique for y_1 and y_4, we obtain the recurrence relations

$$y_1(m) = y_1(m-1) + [\text{if } y_1(m-1) \geqslant y_2(m-1)$$
$$\text{then } -y_2(m-1)$$
$$\text{else } 0] \qquad \text{at } M,$$

and

$$y_4(m) = y_4(m-1) + [\text{if } y_1(m-1) \geqslant y_2(m-1)$$
$$\text{then } y_3(m-1)$$
$$\text{else } 0] \qquad \text{at } M.$$

Writing these equations as a summation, then using (B6) to replace the occurrence of $-y_2(m-1)$ by $-x_2 \cdot y_3(m-1)$ and factoring out $-x_2$, we obtain

$$y_1(m) = y_1(0) - x_2 \cdot \sum_{i=1}^{m} [\text{if } y_1(i-1) \geqslant y_2(i-1)$$
$$\text{then } y_3(i-1)$$
$$\text{else } 0] \qquad \text{at } M,$$

and

$$y_4(m) = y_4(0) + \sum_{i=1}^{m} [\text{if } y_1(i-1) \geqslant y_2(i-1)$$
$$\text{then } y_3(i-1)$$
$$\text{else } 0] \qquad \text{at } M.$$

Combining these formulas, we get

$$y_1(m) - y_1(0) = -x_2 \cdot [y_4(m) - y_4(0)] \quad \text{at } M. \qquad (2.6)$$

We will again use invariants from (B5) at L, namely $y_1 = x_1$ and $y_4 = 0$, to evaluate $y_1(0)$ and $y_4(0)$ at M. There are two possible paths from L to M. If the right branch is used, clearly

$$y_1(0) = x_1 \;\wedge\; y_4(0) = 0 \; \text{at } M.$$

On the other hand, if the left branch is taken, the additional invariants from (B5), $y_1 \leqslant y_2$, $y_2 = x_2 \cdot y_3$ and $y_1 = x_1$ at L, together with the fact that $y_1 \geqslant y_2$ along this path, yield that $y_1 = y_2$ and $y_3 = y_2/x_2 = y_1/x_2 = x_1/x_2$. Therefore, after the assignments $y_1 \leftarrow y_1 - y_2$ and $y_4 \leftarrow y_4 + y_3$, we have that

$y_1(0) = 0$ and $y_4(0) = x_1/x_2$ at M.

Substituting both possibilities for $y_1(0)$ and $y_4(0)$ into the above equation (2.6), we obtain in both cases $y_1(m) - x_1 = -x_2 \cdot y_4(m)$. Thus we have the invariant

(B7) $x_1 = y_4 \cdot x_2 + y_1$ at M.

Turning to the tests, following Equation (2.4) we have
$$m = 0$$
$$\vee \quad [y_3(m-1) \neq 1 \wedge y_1(m-1) \geqslant y_2(m-1)/2] \quad \text{(left path)}$$
$$\vee \quad [y_3(m-1) \neq 1 \wedge y_1(m-1) < y_2(m-1)/2] \quad \text{(right path)}.$$

We try to substitute, using the recurrence equations for the left path in $y_3(m-1) \neq 1 \wedge y_1(m-1) \geqslant y_2(m-1)/2$, and the recurrence equations for the right path in $y_3(m-1) \neq 1 \wedge y_1(m-1) < y_2(m-1)/2$. For the left path, we have the recurrence relations

$$\left.\begin{array}{l} y_1(m) = y_1(m-1) - y_2(m-1)/2 \\ y_2(m) = y_2(m-1)/2 \\ y_3(m) = y_3(m-1)/2 \end{array}\right\} \quad \text{(left path),}$$

and for the right path we have

$$\left.\begin{array}{l} y_1(m) = y_1(m-1) \\ y_2(m) = y_2(m-1)/2 \\ y_3(m) = y_3(m-1)/2 \end{array}\right\} \quad \text{(right path).}$$

Using these equations we obtain
$$m = 0$$
$$\vee \quad [2y_3(m) \neq 1 \wedge y_1(m) \geqslant 0] \qquad \text{(left path)}$$
$$\vee \quad [2y_3(m) \neq 1 \wedge y_1(m) < y_2(m)] \qquad \text{(right path)}.$$

Equivalently, we can write

$$[m = 0 \vee 2y_3(m) \neq 1] \wedge$$
$$[m = 0 \vee y_1(m) \geqslant 0 \vee y_1(m) < y_2(m)]. \tag{2.7}$$

For the first conjunct, we can eliminate the $m = 0$ alternative because by (B5) we have $y_3(0) \geqslant 1$ at M, and therefore $2y_3(0) \neq 1$ at M. We therefore have the invariant

(B8) $2y_3 \neq 1$ at M.

For the second conjunct of (2.7), we can eliminate the $m = 0$ alternative because, as shown earlier, $y_1(0)$ at M is either 0 or x_1, and thus $y_1(m) \geqslant 0$ is true when $m = 0$. We have the invariant

(B9) $y_1 \geqslant 0 \vee y_1 < y_2$ at M.

So far we have used only the algorithmic techniques on the lower block, and have directly generated invariants (B6), (B7), (B8), and (B9) at M. Now we illustrate how some of the heuristic methods could be applied in order to obtain additional invariants.

Turning to the rule of Section 4.1, we consider each disjunct of (B9) separately. It is straightforward to show that both $y_1 \geqslant 0$ and $y_1 < y_2$ are invariants at M; i.e., we may add

(B10) $y_1 \geqslant 0 \wedge y_1 < y_2$ at M.

Using the rule of Section 4.4, we push forward to M the invariants in (B5), and among the candidates obtained is $y_3 \geqslant 1$. Since, using the invariant $y_3 = 2^n/2^m$ from (B6), we prove that for both paths around the loop

$$\forall \bar{y}[y_3 \geqslant 1 \wedge y_3 = 2^n/2^m \wedge y_3 \neq 1 \supset y_3/2 \geqslant 1],$$

we have the new invariant

(B11) $y_3 \geqslant 1$ at M.

(A consequence of (B11) is that $n \geqslant m$ at M.) In turn, (B11) can be used, along with invariants $y_2 = x_2 \cdot 2^n/2^m$ and $y_3 = 2^n/2^m$ from (B6), to show that the candidate $y_2, y_3 \in \{\text{integers}\}$ is an invariant.

We can obtain that y_1, $y_4 \in \{$integers$\}$ by pushing forward the invariants at L; thus

(B12) $y_1, y_2, y_3, y_4 \in \{$integers$\}$ at M.

Observe that if we had used the heuristic of Section 2.3 to push the given output specification at H backwards to M at an early stage, we could have obtained the important candidate invariants $x_1 = y_4 \cdot x_2 + y_1$, $0 \leqslant y_1$, $y_1, y_4 \in \{$integers$\}$, and $y_1 < x_2$ directly by this method. As shown, the first three candidates are indeed invariants at N, while any attempt to establish the fourth candidate $y_1 < x_2$ will fail.

Now, by pushing forward to H the invariants (B6) to (B12) at M, adding the exit test $y_3 = 1$, and simplifying, we obtain the invariants

(B13) $y_3 = 1 \wedge y_2 = x_2 \wedge n = m \wedge x_1 = y_4 \cdot x_2 + y_1 \wedge$

$0 \leqslant y_1 < x_2 \wedge y_1, y_2, y_3, y_4 \in \{$integers$\}$ at H.   □

5. Correctness and Incorrectness

As indicated in the Introduction, invariants may be used to prove the correctness or incorrectness of a program. In order to place these properties in their proper framework, we first present some basic definitions and lemmas [which follow Manna (1969, 1974)].

(a) A program P *terminates over* $\phi(\bar{x})$ if for every input $\bar{a}$ such that $\phi(\bar{a})$ is true, the execution reaches a HALT statement.

(b) A program P is *partially correct w.r.t.* $\phi(\bar{x})$ *and* $\psi(\bar{x}, \bar{y})$ if for every input $\bar{a}$ such that $\phi(\bar{a})$ is true, whenever the program terminates with some $\bar{b}$ as the final value of $\bar{y}$, $\psi(\bar{a}, \bar{b})$ is true.

(c) A program P is *totally correct w.r.t.* $\phi(\bar{x})$ *and* $\psi(\bar{x}, \bar{y})$ if for every input $\bar{a}$ such that $\phi(\bar{a})$ is true, the program terminates with some $\bar{b}$ as the final value of $\bar{y}$ and $\psi(\bar{a}, \bar{b})$ is true.

We are interested in proving that a program is either totally correct *(correct)* or not totally correct *(incorrect)*. We introduce termination and partial correctness because together they are equivalent to total correctness, and, as we shall see, for a proof technique based on invariants it is easier to prove these two properties separately rather than to prove total correctness directly.

The Lemmas B–D and B'–D' (Table 2.1) use the invariants $\{q_h(\overline{x}, \overline{y})\}$ at the haltpoints to provide criteria for proving termination, partial correctness, total correctness, and their negations. For clarity we have used an informal abbreviated notation. Lemma B, for example, should be stated as:

Lemma B. *A program P terminates over ϕ if and only if for every set of invariants $\{q_i(\overline{x}, \overline{y})\}$ and every input $\overline{x}$ such that $\phi(\overline{x})$ is true, there exists a haltpoint h such that $\exists \overline{y}[q_h(\overline{x}, \overline{y})]$ is true.*

Proof. If the program terminates, then for every input $\overline{x}$ satisfying $\phi(\overline{x})$ some haltpoint h must be reached, and $\overline{y}$ will naturally have some value $\overline{b}$ at h. Then, by the definition of an invariant, for every set of invariants, $q_h(\overline{x}, \overline{b})$ must be true, i.e., $\exists \overline{y}[q_h(\overline{x}, \overline{y})]$ is true.

In order to prove the Lemma B in the other direction, we introduce the notion of a *minimal invariant* at cutpoint i, denoted by $m_i(\overline{x}, \overline{y})$. A minimal invariant $m_i(\overline{a}, \overline{b})$ is true for some input $\overline{a}$ satisfying $\phi(\overline{a})$ and for some $\overline{b}$ *if and only if* during execution with input $\overline{a}$ the cutpoint i is reached with $\overline{y} = \overline{b}$. Thus $m_i(\overline{x}, \overline{y})$ denotes the *exact domain* of the $\overline{y}$ values which occur at i during execution of the program with input $\overline{x}$.[3]

Now we assume that for every set of invariants and every $\overline{x}$ such that $\phi(\overline{x})$ is true, there exists a haltpoint h such that $\exists \overline{y}[q_h(\overline{x}, \overline{y})]$ is true. Then, in particular, this is true for the set of minimal invariants. By the definition of minimal invariant, since there exists a $\overline{y}$ such that $m_h(\overline{x}, \overline{y})$ is true, that $\overline{y}$ value actually occurs during execution at the haltpoint h, i.e., h must be reached, and the program must therefore terminate.   □

The other lemmas may be proved by using similar arguments.

The six lemmas of Table 2.1 can be divided into two groups. The first group, Lemmas B', C, and D', are expressed in terms of the existence of a single set of invariants $\{q_i(\overline{x}, \overline{y})\}$ (an "$\exists \overline{q}$ formula"). They therefore may be used to prove nontermination, partial correct-

---

[3] Note that from its definition $m_i(\overline{x}, \overline{y})$ always exists as a predicate; for our purposes it is irrelevant how this predicate is expressed.

TABLE 2.1
Applications of the Invariants $\{q_i(\bar{x}, \bar{y})\}$

Lemma B. P terminates over ϕ if and only if
$$\forall \bar{q} \forall \bar{x} \exists h \exists \bar{y}[q_h(\bar{x}, \bar{y})].$$

Lemma B'. P does not terminate over ϕ if and only if
$$\exists \bar{q} \exists \bar{x} \forall h \forall \bar{y}[\sim q_h(\bar{x}, \bar{y})].$$

Lemma C. P is partially correct w.r.t. ϕ and ψ if and only if
$$\exists \bar{q} \forall \bar{x} \forall h \forall \bar{y}[q_h(\bar{x}, \bar{y}) \supset \psi(\bar{x}, \bar{y})].$$

Lemma C'. P is not partially correct w.r.t. ϕ and ψ if and only if
$$\forall \bar{q} \exists \bar{x} \exists h \exists \bar{y}[q_h(\bar{x}, \bar{y}) \wedge \sim \psi(\bar{x}, \bar{y})].$$

Lemma D. P is (totally) correct w.r.t. ϕ and ψ if and only if
$$\forall \bar{q} \forall \bar{x} \exists h \exists \bar{y}[q_h(\bar{x}, \bar{y}) \wedge \psi(\bar{x}, \bar{y})].$$

Lemma D'. P is incorrect w.r.t. ϕ and ψ if and only if
$$\exists \bar{q} \exists \bar{x} \forall h \forall \bar{y}[q_h(\bar{x}, \bar{y}) \supset \sim \psi(\bar{x}, \bar{y})].$$

$\forall \bar{q}$ means "for every set of invariants $\{q_i(\bar{x}, \bar{y})\}$".
$\exists \bar{q}$ means "there exists a set of invariants $\{q_i(\bar{x}, \bar{y})\}$".
$\forall \bar{x}$ means "for every input $\bar{x}$ such that $\phi(\bar{x})$ is true."
$\exists \bar{x}$ means "there exists an input $\bar{x}$ such that $\phi(\bar{x})$ is true".
$\forall h$ means "for every haltpoint h".
$\exists h$ means "there exists a haltpoint h".

ness, and incorrectness, respectively, by demonstrating a set of invariants which satisfies the appropriate formula. The techniques of Sections 3 and 4 can be used to produce such a set of invariants. Lemmas B, C', and D, on the other hand, are expressed in terms of every possible set of invariants $\{q_i(\bar{x}, \bar{y})\}$ (a "$\forall \bar{q}$ formula"), and may not be used directly with our techniques.

Since total correctness is expressed by a $\forall \bar{q}$ formula, we try to prove this property by showing partial correctness and termination separately. Lemma C uses an $\exists \bar{q}$ formula, and therefore is used to prove partial correctness. This lemma in fact represents "Floyd's method" for proving partial correctness. The problem of termination, however, remains, since it is expressed in terms of a $\forall \bar{q}$ formula. Termination must therefore be treated by other means, which will be discussed at the end of this section.

Incorrectness, on the other hand, is expressed by an $\exists \bar{q}$ formula, and therefore can be proven directly by our techniques, using Lemma D'. Note that the formula of this lemma can be expressed alternatively as

$$\exists \bar{q} \exists \bar{x} \forall h \forall \bar{y}[\sim q_h(\bar{x}, \bar{y}) \vee \sim \psi(\bar{x}, \bar{y})],$$

i.e., for some input $\bar{x}$, either the program does not terminate or the final result is incorrect.

We first illustrate the use of Lemma C for proving partial correctness.

Example B (continued). We would like to show that program B of Figure 2.6 is partially correct w.r.t.

$$\phi(\bar{x}) : x_1 \geqslant 0 \wedge x_2 > 0 \wedge x_1, x_2 \in \{\text{integers}\},$$

and

$$\psi(\bar{x}, \bar{y}) : x_1 = y_4 \cdot x_2 + y_1 \wedge 0 \leqslant y_1 < x_2 \wedge y_1, y_4 \in \{\text{integers}\}.$$

Using invariants (B1) to (B4) at N, (B5) at L, and (B6) to (B12) at M, we have established the invariants (B13) at H (the only haltpoint of the program). Since (B13) contains the invariants

$$x_1 = y_4 \cdot x_2 + y_1 \wedge 0 \leqslant y_1 < x_2 \wedge y_1, y_4 \in \{\text{integers}\},$$

we clearly have that

$$\forall \bar{x} \, \forall \bar{y} [q_H(\bar{x}, \bar{y}) \supset \psi(\bar{x}, \bar{y})].$$

Thus, by Lemma C, program B is partially correct w.r.t. ϕ and ψ. (Note that (B13) actually contains additional information about the final values of the variables, namely that $y_3 = 1$, $y_2 = x_2$, and $n = m$ at the haltpoint H.)   □

Thus, to prove partial correctness, we merely exhibit the invariants at the haltpoints which fulfill Lemma C. On the other hand, in order to prove incorrectness we must provide, in addition to appropriate invariants, an input value $\bar{x}_0$ satisfying $\phi(\bar{x}_0)$ such that the formula in Lemma D$'$ is true. We would like to develop candidates for $\bar{x}_0$ in a systematic manner, similar to the way invariants were generated in Sections 3 and 4. For this reason, it is desirable to find a predicate $\phi'(\bar{x})$ which specifies a nonempty subset of the legal inputs for which the program is incorrect, rather than merely demonstrating the incorrectness for a single $\bar{x}$. That is, to establish incorrectness we prove that for some $\phi'(\bar{x})$,

$$\forall \bar{x} [\phi'(\bar{x}) \supset \phi(\bar{x})] \wedge$$
$$\exists \bar{x} \phi'(\bar{x}) \wedge$$
$$\exists \bar{q} \, \forall \bar{x} \, \forall h \, \forall \bar{y} [\phi'(\bar{x}) \wedge q_h(\bar{x}, \bar{y}) \supset \sim \psi(\bar{x}, \bar{y})].$$

In general, a proof which establishes incorrectness for a large set of input values is also more useful for the diagnosis and correction of the logical errors than an incorrectness proof for a single input value (see Section 6).

We will develop candidates for $\phi'(\overline{x})$ by starting with $\phi(\overline{x})$ and adding conjuncts (restrictions) to $\phi(\overline{x})$ one after another as the need arises. Thus $\phi'(\overline{x}) \supset \phi(\overline{x})$ will be guaranteed true. In case there are several alternative restrictions at some stage of the process, we prefer adding the weakest possible, so that $\phi'(\overline{x})$ will allow maximal freedom in choosing additional restrictions later. At each stage, of course, it is necessary to demonstrate that $\phi'(\overline{x})$ is satisfiable.

Note that all invariants which have been proven for $\phi(\overline{x})$ will remain true for any $\phi'(\overline{x})$ specifying a subset of $\phi(\overline{x})$. Moreover, at each stage of the process we now may discover additional invariants which are true for every $\overline{x}$ satisfying $\phi'(\overline{x})$ but are not necessarily true for every $\overline{x}$ satisfying $\phi(\overline{x})$.

Example A (continued). An attempt to prove the partial correctness of program A (Figure 2.5) will not succeed. Although the invariants (A10) at H can be used to establish $y_4 \leqslant x_1/x_2$ because

$$\forall \overline{x} \forall \overline{y} [y_4 \leqslant x_1/(2x_2) \supset y_4 \leqslant x_1/x_2],$$

we are unable to establish $x_1/x_2 - x_3 < y_4$. Thus we turn to incorrectness, trying to show that for some $\phi'(\overline{x})$ which specifies a nonempty subset of the legal inputs, and for some invariants $q_H(\overline{x}, \overline{y})$ at H, we have

$$\forall \overline{x} \forall \overline{y} [\phi'(\overline{x}) \wedge q_H(\overline{x}, \overline{y}) \supset x_1/x_2 - x_3 \geqslant y_4].$$

We first could try to show that the program is incorrect for *every* legal input $\overline{x}$, i.e., let $\phi'(\overline{x})$ be $\phi(\overline{x})$ itself, but such an attempt will fail. To find a better candidate $\phi'(\overline{x})$, we notice that the "desired" conjunct is $y_4 \leqslant x_1/x_2 - x_3$, and that the invariant $y_4 \leqslant x_1/(2x_2)$ at H of (A10) also provides an upper bound of y_4 in terms of $\overline{x}$. This suggests using the transitivity of inequalities to find an $r(\overline{x})$ such that

$$[y_4 \leqslant x_1/(2x_2) \wedge r(\overline{x})] \supset y_4 \leqslant x_1/x_2 - x_3.$$

The "most general" candidate for $r(\overline{x})$ is clearly $x_1/(2x_2) \leqslant x_1/x_2 - x_3$, or, equivalently,

$$r(\overline{x}) : x_3 \leqslant x_1/(2x_2).$$

The trial $\phi'(\overline{x})$ will therefore be $\phi(\overline{x}) \wedge r(\overline{x})$, i.e.,

$$\phi'(\overline{x}) : 0 \leqslant x_1 < x_2 \wedge 0 < x_3 \wedge x_3 \leqslant x_1/(2x_2).$$

From the development of $\phi'(\overline{x})$, it is obvious that $y_4 \leqslant x_1/x_2 - x_3$ is an invariant at H for every $\overline{x}$ satisfying $\phi'(\overline{x})$. Thus to establish incorrectness it only remains to show that $\phi'(\overline{x})$ is satisfiable. Since we may first choose any x_1 and x_2 such that $0 < x_1 < x_2$, and then choose any x_3 such that $0 < x_3 \leqslant x_1/(2x_2)$, the satisfiability of $\phi'(\overline{x})$ is obvious.   □

Recall that we have not yet provided a practical method for proving termination. The difficulty arose from the fact that Lemma B of Table 2.1 requires proving a "$\forall \overline{q}$ formula". Therefore we clearly need a special method for proving termination.

The traditional method suggested by Floyd (1967) involved choosing a well-founded set $(W, >)$, where $>$ is a partial ordering having the property that there is no infinitely descending chain of elements $w1 > w2 > \cdots$ from W. For every cutpoint i, one must find a partial function $u_i(\overline{x}, \overline{y})$ which maps the elements of the variables' domain into W, and an invariant $q_i(\overline{x}, \overline{y})$ which serves to restrict the domain of u_i. A proof of termination requires showing that each time control moves from cutpoint i to cutpoint j (along a path which includes no other cutpoints and which is a part of some loop), $u_i(\overline{x}, \overline{y}) > u_j(\overline{x}, \overline{y})$. Intuitively, since by definition there is no infinitely decreasing chain of elements in any well-founded set, the proof implies that no execution path of the program can be infinitely long.

The use of Floyd's method entails choosing the appropriate well-founded set $(W, >)$, the functions $\{u_i(\overline{x}, \overline{y})\}$, and the invariants $\{q_i(\overline{x}, \overline{y})\}$. We will suggest an alternative method for proving termination which will be strongly oriented toward the use of invariants, so that we may take advantage of the techniques of Sections 3 and 4. We present the method briefly.

As explained in the Preliminaries section, it is assumed that we can divide the given program into blocks in such a way that every block has only one top-level loop (in addition to possible "lower-level" loops already contained in inner blocks). We treat the inner-most blocks first, and work outwards. Thus, for each block we can consider only its top-level loop (with a unique cutpoint), assuming its inner blocks are known to terminate.

We suggest proving termination of a block with cutpoint i and counter n (assuming that the inner blocks terminate) by finding invariants which will imply that n is absolutely bounded from above at i. That is, $n \leqslant c_i$ at i for some constant c_i. Therefore, the cutpoint cannot be reached infinitely many times during computation. Note that it is actually sufficient to show $a_i(\overline{x}, n) \leqslant b_i(\overline{x})$ where $a_i(\overline{x}, n)$ is an integer-valued function monotonic in n [i.e., if n increases in value, so does $a_i(\overline{x}, n)$]. We therefore state

Lemma E (termination). *A program P terminates if and only if there exists a set of invariants $\{q_i\}$ and functions $\{a_i\}$ and $\{b_i\}$ such that for every block B with cutpoint i and counter n,*

$$\forall \overline{x} \, \forall \overline{y} \, \forall n [q_i(\overline{x}, \overline{y}, n) \supset a_i(\overline{x}, n) \leqslant b_i(\overline{x})], \tag{2.8}$$

where $a_i(\overline{x}, n)$ is an integer-valued function monotonic in n.

The practical importance of the above Lemma E is that we may use invariants which link n to the program variables to derive directly the appropriate functions a_i and b_i. Recall that in such programs, we have the "built-in" invariant that n is a strictly increasing non-negative integer. We shall use these properties in our examples without explicit indication. Although n and $a_i(\overline{x}, n)$ are integers, $b_i(\overline{x})$ can be any number, and the input variables $\overline{x}$ and program variables $\overline{y}$ need not even be numeric; this technique is perfectly applicable to programs with lists, strings, etc. Lemma E can be proved formally by reduction to Floyd's method.

One can weaken the termination condition (2.8) of Lemma E in several different ways. For example, we can often generate $R(\overline{x}, \overline{y})$, the disjunction of the conditions for following a path from Cutpoint i around the loop and back to i in B. We may then use it in proving that the counter in bounded, since if $R(\overline{x}, \overline{y})$ is false, the loop will terminate anyway. Another possibility is to use in a_i and b_i all those variables of $\overline{y}$ (and all those counters), denoted by $\overline{y}'$, which are not changed in B. Thus it actually suffices to prove the weaker condition

$$\forall \overline{x} \, \forall \overline{y} \, \forall n [q_i(\overline{x}, \overline{y}, n) \wedge R(\overline{x}, \overline{y}) \supset a_i(\overline{x}, \overline{y}', n) \leqslant b_i(\overline{x}, \overline{y}')]. \tag{2.9}$$

Example A (continued). Consider again Program A of Figure 2.5. From $\phi(\overline{x})$ and invariant (A2) we note that $0 < x_3 \wedge y_3 = 1/2^n$ is an invariant at N. Thus since

$$\forall \bar{x} \, \forall \bar{y} \, \forall \, n \, [0 < x_3 \wedge y_3 = 1/2^n \wedge y_3 > x_3 \supset 2^n < 1/x_3]$$

is true, it follows by Lemma E that the program terminates over $\phi(\bar{x})$.

□

Example B (continued). Consider Program B of Figure 2.6. Using the known invariant (B1), $y_2 = x_2 \cdot 2^n$ at N, and $\phi(\bar{x})$, we obtain

$$\forall \bar{x} \, \forall \bar{y} \, \forall n \, [x_2 > 0 \wedge y_2 = x_2 \cdot 2^n \wedge y_2 < y_1 \supset 2^n < y_1/x_2].$$

Since y_1 is unchanged in the upper block, it follows by 2.9 that the upper block terminates.

For the lower block we use the invariants (B6) and (B11), $y_3 = 2^n/2^m \wedge y_3 \geqslant 1$ at M, and obtain

$$\forall \bar{x} \, \forall \bar{y} \, \forall n \, \forall m \, [y_3 = 2^n/2^m \wedge y_3 \geqslant 1 \supset 2^m \leqslant 2^n].$$

Since n is unchanged in the lower block, the termination of this block also follows by 2.9.   □

The reader should not be misled into assuming that proving termination is always as trivial as it seems here. The method of Lemma E is examined in greater detail (and presented with some nontrivial examples) in Katz and Manna (1975).

Note that the method of Lemma E, as well as Floyd's original method, is useful only for showing termination. If we want to prove nontermination, both methods are inapplicable (again, *all* possible q_i's must be checked). Thus Lemma B' should be used.

Another important side benefit of using counters lies in the information provided on the time complexity of the given program. By analyzing the invariants at the cutpoints, upper bounds may be obtained on the number of times the loops can be executed. It is sometimes feasible also to discover an invariant of the form $r' \leqslant n$ at a point immediately after the exit from the loop, thus yielding a lower bound on the number of times the loop will be executed.

Example A (continued). Using the invariants (A2) and (A5) of program A (Figure 2.5),

$$y_3 = 1/2^n \quad \text{and} \quad n = 0 \vee 2y_3 > x_3 \quad \text{at } N,$$

we obtain the upper bound $n = 0 \vee 2^n < 2/x_3$.

The exit test and invariant (A2) imply that

$$y_3 = 1/2^n \text{ and } y_3 \leqslant x_3 \quad \text{at } H.$$

Therefore $1/x_3 \leqslant 2^n$ is a lower bound upon exit from the loop. That is, in this program the relations

$$n = 0 \ \lor \ 1/x_3 \leqslant 2^n < 2/x_3$$

are satisfied, and the exact number of executions of the loop can be computed as a function of the input.   □

Example B (continued). In order to obtain an upper bound on the number of executions of the first loop of Program B (Figure 2.6), we need to generate an additional invariant which was not needed previously. Using the technique for generating invariants from tests, we obtain

$$n = 0 \ \lor \ y_1(n - 1) > y_2(n - 1).$$

Since $y_1(n) = y_1(n - 1)$ and $y_2(n) = 2y_2(n - 1)$, the resulting invariant is

$$n = 0 \ \lor \ y_1 > y_2/2 \quad \text{at } N.$$

Using the invariants (B1) and (B3), $y_1 = x_1$ and $y_2 = x_2 \cdot 2^n$ at N, the upper bound $n = 0 \lor 2^n < 2x_1/x_2$ is obtained.

From (B5) we have

$$y_2 = x_2 \cdot 2^n \ \land \ y_1 = x_1 \ \land \ y_1 \leqslant y_2 \quad \text{at } L.$$

This gives a lower bound of $x_1/x_2 \leqslant 2^n$. Thus, for the first loop the relations

$$n = 0 \ \lor \ x_1/x_2 \leqslant 2^n < 2x_1/x_2$$

are satisfied.

Since $n = m$ at H by (B13), it follows that the second loop is executed the same number of times as the first.   □

6. Automatic Debugging

In this section, we suggest a method for debugging based on the invariants generated from the program. The technique we describe uses the invariants and information about how they were generated in order to modify the program systematically.

As explained in the Introduction, failure to prove correctness leaves us unable to decide whether the program is actually incorrect or has merely eluded our efforts to prove its correctness. Two different philosophical approaches to automatic debugging can be applied as soon as we are unable to prove correctness of a program.

Following what may be termed the *conservative approach,* we would insist on a proof of incorrectness before proceeding to modify the program. This is a reasonable view, and, as will be indicated below, a proof of incorrectness can aid in debugging. The method presented for proving incorrectness of programs was motivated by this approach.

However, proofs of incorrectness are often difficult to obtain, in particular for subtle errors, since the needed $\phi'(\overline{x})$ (a class of inputs leading to incorrectness) must be produced. Thus an alternative to the conservative approach, a *radical approach,* can also be justified. In this approach, we will "fix" the program so that a proof of correctness is guaranteed to succeed, even without having proven that the original program is incorrect. In effect, under this approach we modify a program we merely *suspect* of being incorrect, taking the risk of modifying an already correct program.

The basic debugging technique using invariants is common to both approaches. We shall first describe the technique as it is used in the radical approach. The slight differences which arise if the conservative approach has been used (i.e., if a proof of incorrectness is available) are pointed out later in this section. At the end of the section we briefly compare the two approaches.

For simplicity we will again deal with a simplified model: a single block having no inner blocks, with a cutpoint L at the entrance, N inside the loop, and M at the exit, as in Figure 2.3 or 2.4. In addition to the candidates produced and invariants proven for each cutpoint during the process of invariant generation, we assume candidates $s''(\overline{x}, \overline{y})$ at M which would guarantee partial correctness of the program were they actually invariants. For the case in which M is a haltpoint, $s''(\overline{x}, \overline{y})$ would naturally be the output specification itself.

To effectively use the invariants for debugging, it is necessary to record in an *invariant table* all the information required to establish each invariant, e.g., the rule applied, and precisely how the program statements and other invariants were used in its derivation. In addition, the uses of that invariant for proving other invariants must be noted. In general there will be an entire invariant table associated with each cutpoint. However, there is usually an essential difference in the complexity of the table for cutpoints on a loop, like N, and for those not on a loop, like M. All of the invariants at M, for example, will be obtained simply by "pushing forward" either invariants at N or the exit condition of the block. Thus below we concentrate on the more interesting case of the invariant table at N.

For clarity, we will use a more pictorial representation for the invariant table at N and arrange the invariants generated in the form of a directed acyclic graph (dag). We use terminology similar to that of trees, talking about the "ancestors" or "descendants" of an invariant, and of moving "up" or "down" the graph, and we refer to the graph as an *invariant tree*. We will have invariants from previous blocks given in $p(\overline{x},\overline{y})$, the initial assignment statements of the block, and the statements of the loop at the top of the tree. Each invariant $q(\overline{x}, \overline{y})$ at N is the descendant of the loop statements, initial assignments, and other invariants used to establish $q(\overline{x}, \overline{y})$.

By examining such an invariant tree, we can see both how a desired change in any given statement will affect the various invariants, and (conversely) how a desired change in an invariant can be achieved by changing statements.

The basic steps in correcting the program are as follows (again referring to Figures 2.3 or 2.4):

1. Using the heuristic methods of Section 4, such as 4.3, generate candidates for invariants $q''(\overline{x}, \overline{y})$ at N which would allow proving the candidates $s''(\overline{x}, \overline{y})$ at M to be invariants, and thus would allow proving partial correctness.[4] It is also possible to generate candidate exit tests $t'(\overline{x}, \overline{y})$ or candidate exit functions $h'(\overline{x}, \overline{y})$ which would guarantee partial correctness along with the existing invariants at N. In the continuation, we discuss changing only the invariants at N, although similar considerations apply to changing the exit test or exit function.

---

[4] The possibility that the program is partially correct but nonterminating will not be treated in our discussion; actually it would lead to a correcting process similar to that described here.

2. Find actual invariants $q(\bar{x}, \bar{y})$ in the invariant tree which are "similar" to those candidates $q''(\bar{x}, \bar{y})$ which guarantee correctness. The precise definition given to "similarity" will have a direct influence on the kinds of errors which may be corrected, and there are obviously many possibilities. We here assume that two predicates are *similar* if they differ only in constant (non-zero) coefficients of variables, a constant term, or other minor perturbations in the relation involved, such as $<$ in place of $\leqslant$. When we have succeeded in finding invariants $q(\bar{x}, \bar{y})$ in the tree similar to candidates $q''(\bar{x}, \bar{y})$, the candidates will be called the *goal candidates* at N, and denoted $q^*(\bar{x}, \bar{y})$.

3. Attempt to replace $q(\bar{x}, \bar{y})$ by the similar goal candidates $q^*(\bar{x}, \bar{y})$, moving up the tree and modifying the ancestors of $q(\bar{x}, \bar{y})$ so that the new $q^*(\bar{x}, \bar{y})$ will be derived rather than the former $q(\bar{x}, y)$.

4. When a *statement* has been modified in order to allow deriving a goal candidate, inspect (by moving down the tree) the effect of the modification on all other invariants derived from it. This is necessary in order to ensure that no other part of the proof of partial correctness or the proof of termination is disturbed. The inspection could require making additional "compensatory" changes in other statements, or abandoning a possible change.

Example A (continued). Consider once again Program A of Figure 2.5. The invariant tree for the program is shown in Figure 2.7. For simplicity, we have merely listed the number of the rule which was applied to obtain each invariant, rather than including more information. A brief review of the generation of invariants for this example (in Sections 3 and 4) should make the tree clear [except for (A11), which should be momentarily ignored]. We have added the "termination" and "partial correctness" boxes at the bottom of the tree to emphasize which statements and invariants were used to prove termination (with bound $2^n < 1/x_3$) and partial correctness (w.r.t. $y_4 \leqslant x_1/x_2$). Recall that we were unable to prove partial correctness for $x_1/x_2 - x_3 < y_4$, the first conjunct of the output specification. In order to demonstrate the radical approach, we momentarily ignore the fact that in Section 5 we actually have proven this program incorrect.

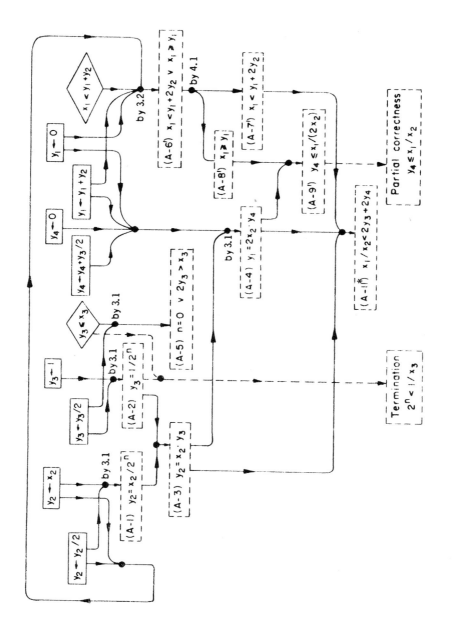

Figure 2.7. The Invariant Tree for Cutpoint N of Program A.

The problematic part of the output specification, $x_1/x_2 - x_3 < y_4$, is automatically a candidate invariant at H. Using the heuristic of Section 4.3, we can generate candidate invariants at N by pushing back the candidate at H (assuming temporarily that the exit test $y_3 \leqslant x_3$ is correct). The strongest candidate at N is $x_1/x_2 - x_3 < y_4$ itself. We may also use the transitivity of inequalities with $x_1/x_2 - x_3 < y_4$ and the exit condition $y_3 \leqslant x_3$ to suggest another natural candidate. We need a $q(\bar{x}, \bar{y})$ such that

$$q(\bar{x}, \bar{y}) \wedge y_3 \leqslant x_3 \supset x_1/x_2 - y_4 < x_3,$$

and see easily that the most general $q(\bar{x}, \bar{y})$ which will do this is $x_1/x_2 - y_4 < y_3$, or $x_1/x_2 < y_3 + y_4$.

Naturally, if either of these candidates could be proven to be an invariant at N, the program already would have been proven correct. Now we turn to the invariant tree in order to modify the program so that a correctness proof is possible. We look for invariants already in the tree which are similar to the above candidates, and also try to combine existing invariants into new ones similar to the candidates.

For the candidate $x_1/x_2 - x_3 < y_4$, we find no similar invariant. For the second candidate, $x_1/x_2 < y_3 + y_4$, we may combine (A3), (A4), and (A7), giving

$$[y_2 = x_2 \cdot y_3 \ \wedge \ y_1 = 2x_2 \cdot y_4 \ \wedge \ x_1 < y_1 + 2y_2] \supset$$
$$x_1/x_2 < 2y_3 + 2y_4, \qquad\qquad (2.10)$$

i.e., we have the new invariant

(A11) $x_1/x_2 < 2y_3 + 2y_4$ at N.

This is similar to the candidate, which we now will refer to as the goal candidate

(A11*) $x_1/x_2 < y_3 + y_4$ at N.

We have thus found a place to "hang" the candidate on the tree, and now must adjust the ancestors of (A11) [i.e., (A3), (A4), or (A7)] so that (A11*) will be derived instead. By examining Equation (2.10), it is not difficult to see that two of the most direct modifications among the many possibilities are

(a) leave (A3) and (A4) unchanged, but change

$$(A7) \ x_1 < y_1 + 2y_2 \ \text{ to } \ (A7') \ 2x_1 < y_1 + 2y_2 \,;$$

or

(b) leave (A7) unchanged, but change

$$(A3) \ y_2 = x_2 \cdot y_3 \ \text{ to } \ (A3') \ 2y_2 = x_2 \cdot y_3$$

and

$$(A4) \ y_1 = 2x_2 \cdot y_4 \ \text{ to } \ (A4') \ y_1 = x_2 \cdot y_4 \,.$$

Possibility (a) will be considered first. The invariant tree shows that (A7) was derived from the invariant

$$(A6) \ x_1 < y_1 + 2y_2 \ \vee \ x_1 \geqslant y_1 \ \text{at } N,$$

by using the Disjunct Elimination Rule of Section 4.1 to strengthen the invariant. To obtain (A7'), we will first modify (A6) to

$$(A6') \ 2x_1 < y_1 + 2y_2 \ \vee \ h(\overline{x}, \overline{y}),$$

where $h(\overline{x}, \overline{y})$ is the part of (A6') not of interest to us at the moment. By tracing back through the derivation of (A6) (which used the algorithmic rule of Section 3.2), the left alternative of (A6) can be seen to originate as

(i) $x_1 < y_1(n-1) + y_2(n-1)$

(from the test $x_1 < y_1 + y_2$, using the right path),

(ii) $y_1(n) = y_1(n-1)$

(from the fact that y_1 is unchanged along the right path),

(iii) $y_2(n) = y_2(n-1)/2$

(from the assignment $y_2 \leftarrow y_2/2$).

These clearly were combined to yield the alternative $x_1 < y_1 + 2y_2$.

To obtain $2x_1 < y_1 + 2y_2$ instead, we replace (i) by $2x_1 < y_1(n-1) + y_2(n-1)$, i.e., change the test statement $x_1 < y_1 + y_2$ to $2x_1 < y_1 + y_2$. This suggested change was built to yield an acceptable left alternative of (A6'). Checking $2x_1 < y_1 + 2y_2$ alone, we may conclude that with this suggested change (A7') is indeed an invariant, and thus, so is the goal (A11*).

We must now check whether any other vital invariants are affected. From the tree it is clear that the only effect could be on the right alternative of (A6) and its descendants. Using the new test statement, it is easy to see that the left path leads to

$$2x_1 \geqslant y_1(n-1) + y_2(n-1)$$

(from the test $2x_1 < y_1 + y_2$, using the left path),

$$y_1(n) = y_1(n-1) + y_2(n-1)$$

(from the assignment $y_1 \leftarrow y_1 + y_2$ on the left path).

These clearly combine to yield $2x_1 \geqslant y_1(n)$, so that $h(\bar{x}, \bar{y})$ is $2x_1 \geqslant y_1$, and we have the invariant

(A6') $2x_1 < y_1 + 2y_2 \ \lor \ 2x_1 \geqslant y_1$ at N.

Examining the descendants of (A6'), we can see that (A8) must be replaced by

(A8') $2x_1 \geqslant y_1$ at N,

which is an invariant of the modified program. In turn, this combined with (A4) will yield the invariant

(A9') $y_4 \leqslant x_1/x_2$ at N.

Thus we also have the invariant $y_4 \leqslant x_1/x_2$ instead of $y_4 \leqslant x_1/(2x_2)$ at H.

However, this invariant serves just as well as the original $y_4 \leqslant x_1/(2x_2)$ to guarantee partial correctness for the output specification $y_4 \leqslant x_1/x_2$. Thus the suggested correction leads to the goal (A11*)

and does not disturb any other aspect of the proof of correctness, i.e., the modified program is guaranteed correct. In Figure 2.8 we show the invariant tree at N of the modified program, which is totally correct. Thus, to summarize:

Replace the test $x_1 < y_1 + y_2$ *by* $2x_1 < y_1 + y_2$.

Possibility (b) for achieving the goal (A11*) will now be considered, i.e. we would like to replace (A3) and (A4) by (A3′) and (A4′), respectively (again referring to the original invariant tree of Figure 2.7). We immediately note that since (A3) is an ancestor of (A4), any change in (A3) will influence (A4). The invariant (A4) was obtained by bringing two summations involving **if-then-else** to an identical form, so that y_1 and y_4 could be connected. If during the manipulations of the relations, $2y_2 = x_2 \cdot y_3$ is used for substitution instead of $y_2 = x_2 \cdot y_3$, the new (A4) becomes exactly $y_1 = x_2 \cdot y_4$, i.e., the (A4′) we require. Thus if we can change (A3) to (A3′), we "automatically" have changed (A4) to (A4′).

Examining the invariant tree, it is clear that we may achieve (A3′) by changing either (A1) or (A2), i.e., either

(A1) $y_2 = x_2/2^n$ to (A1′) $y_2 = x_2/2^{n+1}$

or

(A2) $y_3 = 1/2^n$ to (A2′) $y_3 = 2/2^n$.

Since $y_2 = y_2(0)/2^n$ and $y_2(0) = x_2$, the first possibility can be achieved by letting $y_2(0) = x_2/2$, i.e., by changing the initialization $y_2 \leftarrow x_2$ to $y_2 \leftarrow x_2/2$. Now we check the possible effect of this change on other invariants. This initialization was used to establish (A6) and (A7) the first time N is reached, but the new initialization also does the same job. Tracing other paths down from this suggested change, we see that (A4) was used to establish $y_4 \leqslant x_1/(2x_2)$ at H. However, the new (A4′), $y_1 = x_2 \cdot y_4$, may still be combined with (A8), $y_1 \leqslant x_1$, to show that $y_4 \leqslant x_1/x_2$ at N and thus at H. Therefore this change is also safe, and we have

Replace the initialization $y_2 \leftarrow x_2$ *by* $y_2 \leftarrow x_2/2$.

The change in (A2), from $y_3 = 1/2^n$ to $y_3 = 2/2^n$, is also easy to achieve, since $y_3 = y_3(0)/2^n$. Thus we set $y_3(0) = 2$ instead of

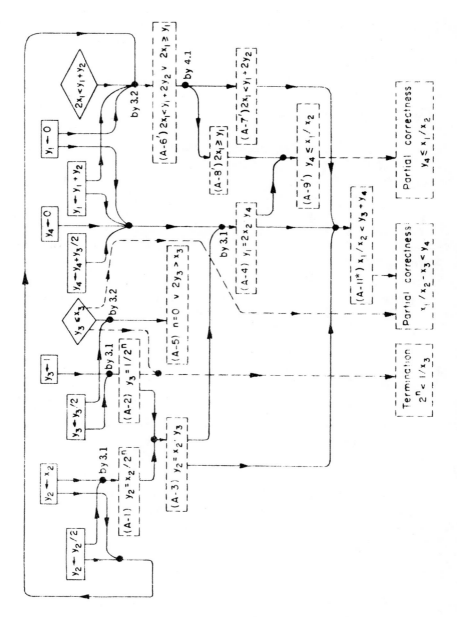

**Figure 2.8. The Invariant Tree for Cutpoint N of the
Modified Program A (correction 1).**

$y_3(0) = 1$, i.e., change the initialization $y_3 \leftarrow 1$ to $y_3 \leftarrow 2$. This change will slightly affect the termination, but the counter n can now be bounded by $2^n < 2/x_3$. Again (A4$'$) can be shown not to disturb the correctness for $y_4 \leqslant x_1/x_2$. Thus a third safe change is

Replace the initialization $y_3 \leftarrow 1$ by $y_3 \leftarrow 2$.   □

So far in this section, we have ignored the possibility that we have already proven the program incorrect. Now we briefly consider how a proof of incorrectness can aid in the automatic debugging process described above.

We assume that when unable to prove correctness, the conservative approach was followed and a proof of incorrectness was produced. Although the existence of this proof has surprisingly little effect on the basic debugging technique, it can be of some aid. Clearly, any change in the program which is intended to correct the error must change at least one of the invariants used in the incorrectness proof. Thus the paths up the tree from the goal candidate can be restricted to those which will influence invariants from the proof of incorrectness. This is valuable because one of the difficulties with the use of the tree is the need for further guidance in the selection of likely paths.

Example A (continued). Let us review the proof of incorrectness of program A of Figure 2.5. We used the invariant $y_4 \leqslant x_1/(2x_2)$ at H [one of the invariants of (A10)] to find an $r(\bar{x})$ such that

$$[y_4 \leqslant x_1/(2x_2) \; \wedge \; r(\bar{x})] \; \supset \; y_4 \leqslant x_1/x_2 - x_3.$$

This suggested taking $r(\bar{x}) : x_1/(2x_2) \leqslant x_1/x_2 - x_3$, since

$$[y_4 \leqslant x_1/(2x_2) \; \wedge \; x_1/(2x_2) \leqslant x_1/x_2 - x_3] \; \supset$$
$$y_4 \leqslant x_1/x_2 - x_3. \tag{2.11}$$

This $r(\bar{x})$ then led to

$$\phi'(\bar{x}) : 0 \leqslant x_1 < x_2 \wedge 0 < x_3 \wedge x_1/(2x_2) \leqslant x_1/x_2 - x_3$$

which was then simplified and shown to be satisfiable.

Now $y_4 \leqslant x_1/(2x_2)$ at H was the only invariant used in the proof of incorrectness and was obtained directly from the invariant (A9), $y_4 \leqslant x_1/(2x_2)$ at N. Thus it follows that any correction of the program *must* change invariant (A9).   □

Let us briefly compare the two approaches.

Because we guarantee correctness, the "radical" approach of modifying without first proving incorrectness is not as dangerous as it might seem. In fact, the only objection would seem to be that in the case of a program which actually was originally correct, the efficiency of execution may be reduced in a modified (also correct) version. From our experience with hand simulations, we believe that *if* we are able to find goal candidates similar to the invariants, the program is very likely incorrect, and it is worthwhile to follow the radical approach without first proving incorrectness.

However, for programs with a large number of errors (or a small number of very gross errors), it is unlikely that the required similarity will be found. "Gross" errors could actually be defined as those which lead to invariants completely irrelevant to a proof of the specification.

In any case, the proof of incorrectness would be a valuable aid to the user, even if an automatic correction could not be made. It provides what could be called *logical diagnostics* about the program. From the conjuncts of the output specification which were contradicted, the general effect of the error is obtained. From $\phi'(\overline{x})$, the user obtains a class of inputs for which the program is incorrect. Most important, from the invariants directly used in the proof of incorrectness, the user can identify the problematic relations in the program.

7. Conclusion

In this paper we have presented an overview of how invariants can be produced and used. The basic concept of an invariant is, of course, not new. We have, however, tried to present a new perspective which shifts emphasis from the limited task of verifying a correct program to the more general framework of logical analysis. From our point of view, invariants are independent entities which can be used for many purposes, of which proving partial correctness is only one.

Numerous improvements and refinements are clearly possible to the invariant-generating techniques presented. In particular, it is necessary to further guide the heuristics in Section 4, so that they will not be applied indiscriminately. For example, only when the need for an invariant involving certain variables has become evident, should candidates involving those variables be generated.

The general problem of generating invariants for a given program is unsolvable. Programs clearly exist with relations among the variables based implicitly on deep mathematical theorems which could not conceivably be rediscovered by any general invariant-generating algorithm.

In a practical implementation, the user would be encouraged to provide his own ideas about what the intermediate invariants should be ("comments"), and these will automatically be considered as candidate invariants. The system could also ask the user to provide suggestions as the need arises for invariants involving specific problematic variables with unclear relationships at a certain cutpoint. We expect that a reasonably sophisticated system based on the techniques presented here, with some aid from the user whenever necessary, could produce sufficient invariants to conduct the logical analysis of some nontrivial programs.

Several other efforts have been made to attack the problem of finding assertions which prove partial correctness. The earliest work was by Floyd (private communications, 1967) and Cooper (1971). Elspas (1974) was the first to consider using recurrence relations. Wegbreit (1974) has developed independently some rules similar to our heuristic approach, and a method using a "weak interpretation" of the program. Katz and Manna (1973) suggested additional heuristics to treat arrays. Greif and Waldinger (1974) also described a method for generating assertions which moves backwards from the output specification.

The idea of adding variables, such as counters, to the program in order to facilitate proofs of partial correctness or termination is not new. Knuth (1968) uses a "time clock" incremented at every statement to prove termination. Elspas et al. (1973) also discuss how such counters can be used in termination proofs. Other related work on termination is that of Cooper (1971) and Sites (1974).

The possibility of using a program verifier to debug programs was first discussed informally by King (1970). Sussman (1975) stresses the importance of systematically eliminating bugs in the context of program synthesis. An attempt to establish incorrectness by finding counterexamples was outlined by Floyd (1971) as part of his proposed system for interactive program writing.

In our presentation we have basically considered the debugging of a program with a single loop. For more complicated programs, with multiple loops, additional research problems present themselves. What we have introduced here is clearly just a first step toward the use of invariants in debugging.

Acknowledgment

We are indebted to Ed Ashcroft, Nachum Dershowitz, Barnard Elspas, Stephen Ness, Tim Standish, and Richard Waldinger for their critical reading of the manuscript.

Chapter 3
Knowledge and Reasoning in Program Synthesis

Zohar Manna and Richard Waldinger

1. Introduction

In this paper we describe some of the knowledge and the reasoning ability that a system must have in order to construct computer programs automatically. We believe that such a system needs to embody a relatively small class of reasoning and programming tactics combined with a great deal of knowledge about the world. These tactics and this knowledge are expressed both procedurally (i.e., explicity in the description of a problem-solving process) and structurally (i.e., implicitly in the choice of representation). We consider the ability to reason as central to the program synthesis process, and most of this paper is concerned with the incorporation of common-sense reasoning techniques into a program synthesis system.

We regard program synthesis as a part of artificial intelligence. Many of the abilities we require of a program synthesizer, such as the ability to represent knowledge or to draw common-sense conclusions from facts, we would also expect from a natural-language understanding system or a robot problem solver. These general problems have been under study by researchers for many years, and we do not expect that they will all be solved in the near future. However, we still prefer to address these problems rather than

This is a revised version of a previously published article by the same name which appeared in *Artificial Intelligence,* vol. 6, pp. 175–208. Copyright 1975 by North-Holland Publishing Company, Amsterdam. Reprinted by permission of publisher.

restrict ourselves to a more limited program synthesis system without those abilities.

Thus, although implementation of some of the techniques in this paper has already been completed, others require further development before a complete implementation will be possible. We imagine the knowledge and reasoning tactics of the system to be expressed in a PLANNER-type language (Hewitt, 1971); our own implementation is in the QLISP language (Wilber, 1976). Further details on the implementation are discussed in Section 5.1.

Section 2 of the paper gives the basic techniques of reasoning for program synthesis. They include the formation of conditional tests and loops, the satisfaction of several simultaneous goals, and the handling of instructions with side effects. Section 3 applies the techniques of Section 2 to synthesize a nontrivial "patternmatcher" that determines whether a given expression is an instance of a given pattern. Section 4 demonstrates the modification of programs. We take the pattern matcher we have constructed in Section 3 and adapt it to construct a more complex program; a "unification algorithm" that determines whether two patterns have a common instance. In Section 5 we give some of the historical background of automatic program synthesis, and we compare this work with other recent efforts.

2. Fundamental Reasoning

In this section we will describe some of the reasoning and programming tactics that are basic to the operation of our proposed synthesizer. These tactics are not specific to one particular domain; they apply to any programming problem. In this class of tactics, we include the formation of program branches and loops and the handling of statements with side effects.

2.1. Specification and Tactics Language

We must first say something about how programming problems are to be specified. In this discussion we consider only correct and exact specifications in an artificial language. Thus, we will not discuss input-output examples [cf. Hardy (1975), Summers (1976)], traces [cf. Biermann and Krishnaswamy (1976)], or natural-language descriptions as methods for specifying programs: nor will we consider interactive specification of programs [cf. Balzer (1972)]. Neither are we limiting ourselves to the first-order predicate calculus [cf. Kowalski (1974)]. Instead, we try to introduce specification constructs that allow the natural and intuitive description of programming problems. We therefore include constructs such as

$$\text{Find } x \text{ such that } P(x)$$

and the ellipsis notation, e.g.,

$$A[1], A[2], ..., A[n].$$

Furthermore, we introduce new constructs that are specific to certain subject domains. For instance, in the domain of sets we use

$$\{x \mid P(x)\}$$

for "the set of all x such that $P(x)$". As we introduce an example we will describe features of the language that apply to that example. Since the specification language is extendible, we can introduce new constructs at any time.

We use a separate language to express the system's knowledge and reasoning tactics. In the paper, these will be expressed in the form of rules written in English. In our implementation, the same rules are represented as programs in the QLISP programming language. When a problem or goal is presented to the system, the appropriate rules are summoned by "pattern-directed function invocation" (Hewitt, 1971). In other words, the form of the goal determines which rules are applied.

In the following two sections we will use a single example, the synthesis of the set-theoretic union program to illustrate the formation both of conditionals and of loops. The problem here is to compute the union of two finite sets, where sets are represented as lists with no repeated elements.

Given two sets, s and t, we want to express

$$union(s \ t) = \{x \mid x \in s \text{ or } x \in t\}$$

in a LISP-like language. We expect the output of the synthesized program to be a set itself. Thus

$$union((A \ B) \ (B \ C)) = (A \ B \ C).$$

We do not regard the expression $\{x \mid x \in s \text{ or } x \in t\}$ itself as a proper program: the operator $\{ \ | \ ...\}$ is a construct in our specification language but not in our LISP-like programming language. We assume that the programming language does have the following functions:

$head(l)$ = the first element of the list l. Thus $head((A \ B \ C \ D)) = A$.
$tail(l)$ = the list of all but the first element of the list l. Thus $tail((A \ B \ C \ D)) = (B \ C \ D)$.[1]
$add(x \ s)$ = the set consisting of the element x and the elements of the set s. Thus $add(A \ (B \ C \ D)) = (A \ B \ C \ D)$ whereas $add(B \ (B \ C \ D)) = (B \ C \ D)$.
$empty(s)$ is true if s is the empty list, and false otherwise.

Our task is to transform the specification for *union* into an equivalent algorithm in this programming language.

We assume the system has some basic knowledge about sets, such as the following rules:

(1) $x \in s$ is false if $empty(s)$.
(2) s is equal to $add(head(s) \ tail(s))$ if $\sim empty(s)$.
(3) $x \in add(s \ t)$ is equivalent to $(x = s$ or $x \in t)$.
(4) $\{x \mid x \in s\}$ is equal to s.
(5) $\{x \mid x = a$ or $Q(x)\}$ is equal to $add(a \ \{x \mid Q(x)\})$.

We also assume that the system knows a considerable amount of propositional logic, which we will not mention explicitly.

Before proceeding with our example we must discuss the formation of conditional expressions.

2.2. Formation of Conditional Expressions

In addition to the above constructs, we assume that our programming language contains conditional expressions of the form

$$(\text{if } p \text{ then } q \text{ else } r) = \begin{cases} r & \text{if } p \text{ is false,} \\ q & \text{otherwise.} \end{cases}$$

The conditional expression is a technique for dealing with uncer-

---

[1] Since sets are represented as lists, *head* and *tail* may be applied to sets as well as lists. Their value then depends on our actual choice of representation.

tainty. Suppose, in constructing a program, we want to know if condition p is true or false, when in fact p may be true on some occasions and false on others, depending on the values of the program's arguments. The human programmer faced with this problem is likely to resort to "hypothetical reasoning": he will assume p is false and write a program r that solves his program in that case; then he will assume p is true and write a program q that works in that case; he will then put the two programs together into a single program

$$(\text{if } p \text{ then } q \text{ else } r).$$

Conceptually he has solved his problem by splitting his world into two worlds: the case in which p is true and the case in which p is false. In each of these worlds, uncertainty is reduced. Note that we must be careful that the condition p on which we are splitting the world is computable in our programming language; otherwise, the conditional expression we construct also will not be computable.

We can now proceed with the synthesis of the union function. Our specifications were

$$union(s\ t) = \{x \mid x \in s \text{ or } x \in t\}.$$

We begin to transform these specifications using our rules. Rule (1) applies to the subexpression $x \in s$, generating a subgoal, $empty(s)$. We cannot prove s is empty—this depends on the input—and therefor e this is an occasion for a hypothetical world split. (We know that $empty(s)$ is a computable condition because $empty$ is a primitive in our language.) In the case in which s is empty, the expression

$$\{x \mid x \in s \text{ or } x \in t\}$$

therefore reduces to

$$\{x \mid \text{false or } x \in t\},$$

or, by propositional logic,

$$\{x \mid x \in t\}.$$

Now rule (4) reduces this to t, which is one of the inputs to our program and therefore is itself an acceptable program segment in our language.

In the other world—the case in which s is not empty—we cannot solve the problem without resorting to the recursive loop formation mechanism, which is the subject of the next section. However, we know at this point that the program will have the form

$$union(s\ t) = \text{if } empty(s)$$
$$\text{then } t$$
$$\text{else. . .,}$$

where the else clause will be whatever program segment we construct for the case in which s is not empty.

2.3. Formation of Loops

The term "loop" includes both iteration and recursion; however, in this paper we will only discuss recursive loops [cf. Manna and Waldinger (1971)]. Intuitively, we form a recursive call when, in the course of working on our problem, we generate a subgoal that is identical in form to our top-level goal. For instance, suppose our top-level goal is to construct the program $reverse(l)$ that reverses the elements of the list l [e.g., $reverse(A\ (B\ C)\ D)=(D\ (B\ C)\ A)$]. If in the course of constructing this program we generate the subgoal of reversing the elements of the list $tail(l)$, we can use the program we are constructing to satisfy this subgoal. In other words, we can introduce a recursive call $reverse(tail(l))$ to solve the subsidiary problem. We must always check that a recursive call does not lead to an infinite recursion. No such infinite loop can occur here, because the input $tail(l)$ is "shorter" than the original input l.

Let us see how the technique applies to our union example. Continuing where we left off in the discussion of conditionals, we attempt to expand the expression

$$\{x \mid x \in s \text{ or } x \in t\}$$

in the case in which s is not empty. Applying rule (2) to the subexpression s, we can expand our expression to

$$\{x \mid x \in add(head(s)\ tail(s)) \text{ or } x \in t\}.$$

This is transformed by rule (3) into

$$\{x \mid x = head(s) \text{ or } x \in tail(s) \text{ or } x \in t\}.$$

Using rule (5), this reduces to

$$add(head(s)\ \{x \mid x \in tail(s) \text{ or } x \in t\}).$$

If we observe that
$$\{x \mid x \in tail(s) \text{ or } x \in t\}$$
is an instance of the top-level subgoal, we can reduce it to
$$union(tail(s) \ t).$$

Again, this recursive call leads to no infinite loops, since *tail(s)* is shorter than *s*. Our completed union program is now

$$union(s \ t) = \text{if } empty(s)$$
$$\text{then } t$$
$$\text{else } add(head(s) \quad union(tail(s) \ t)).$$

As presented in this section, the loop formation technique can only be applied if a subgoal is generated that is a special case of the top-level goal. We shall see in the next section how this restriction can be relaxed.

2.4. Generalization of Specifications

When proving a theorem by mathematical induction, it is often necessary to strengthen the theorem in order for the induction to "go through". Even though we have an apparently more difficult theorem to prove, the proof is facilitated because we have a stronger induction hypothesis. For example, in proving theorems about LISP programs, the theorem prover of Boyer and Moore (1975) often automatically generalizes the statement of the theorem in the course of a proof by induction.

A similar phenomenon occurs in the synthesis of a recursive program. It is often necessary to strengthen the specifications of a program in order for that program to be useful in recursive calls. We believe that this ability to strengthen specifications is an essential part of the synthesis process, as many of our examples will show.

For example, suppose we want to construct a program to reverse a list. A good recursive *reverse* program is
$$reverse(l) = rev(l \ ()),$$
where

$$rev(l \ m) = \text{if } empty(l)$$
$$\text{then } m$$
$$\text{else } rev(tail(l) \ head(l) \cdot m).$$

Here () is the empty list, and $x \cdot l$ is the list formed by inserting x before the first element of the list l [e.g., $A \cdot (B\ C\ D) = (A\ B\ C\ D)$]. Note that $rev(l\ m)$ reverses the list l and appends it onto the list m, e.g.,

$$rev((A\ B\ C)\ (D\ E\ )) = (C\ B\ A\ D\ E).$$

This is a good way to compute *reverse*: it uses very primitive LISP functions, and its recursion is such that it can be compiled without the use of a stack. However, writing such a program entails writing the function *rev*, which is apparently more general and difficult to compute than *reverse* itself, since it must reverse its first argument as a subtask. Actually, the more general program *rev* is easier to construct, and the synthesis of the reverse function involves generalizing the original specifications of *reverse* into the specifications of *rev*.

The *reverse* function requires that the top-level goal be generalized in order to match the lower-level goal. Another way to strengthen the specifications is to propose additional requirements for the program being constructed. For instance, suppose in the course of the synthesis of a function $f(x)$, we generate a subgoal of the form $P(f(a))$, where $f(a)$ is a particular recursive call. If we cannot prove $P(f(a))$, it may still be possible to strengthen the specifications for $f(x)$ so as to also satisfy $P(f(x))$ for all x. This step may require that we actually modify portions of the program f that have already been synthesized in order to satisfy the new specification P. The recursive call to the modified program will then be sure to satisfy $P(f(a))$. This process will be illustrated in more detail during the synthesis of the pattern matcher in Section 3.

The recursion-introduction mechanism presented here has been developed independently by Burstall and Darlington (1977).

2.5. Conjunctive Goals

The problem of solving conjunctive goals is the problem of constructing an output that satisfies two (or more) constraints. The general form for this problem is

Find z such that $P(z)$ and $Q(z)$.

The conjunctive-goal problem is difficult because, even if we have methods for solving the goals

$$\text{Find } z \text{ such that } P(z)$$

and

$$\text{Find } z \text{ such that } Q(z)$$

independently, the two solutions may not merge together nicely into a single solution. Moreover, there seems to be no way of solving the conjunctive-goal problem in general; a method that works on one such problem may be irrelevant to another.

We will illustrate one instance of the conjunctive-goal problem: the solution of two simultaneous linear equations. Although this problem is not itself a program synthesis problem, it could be re-phrased as one. Moreover, the difficulties involved and the technique to be applied extend to many real synthesis problems, such as the pattern-matcher synthesis of Section 3. Suppose our problem is the following:

$$\text{Find } \langle z_1, z_2 \rangle \text{ such that } 2z_1 = z_2 + 1 \text{ and } 2z_2 = z_1 + 2.$$

Suppose further that although we can solve single linear equations with ease, we have no built-in package for solving sets of equations simultaneously. We may try first to find a solution to each equation separately. Solving the first equation, we might come up with

$$\langle z_1, z_2 \rangle = \langle 1, 1 \rangle,$$

whereas solving the second equation might give

$$\langle z_1, z_2 \rangle = \langle 2, 2 \rangle.$$

There is no way of combining these two solutions. Furthermore, it does not help matters to reverse the order in which we approach the two subgoals. What is necessary is to make the solution of the first goal as general as possible, so that some special case of the solution might satisfy the second goal as well. For instance, a "general" solution to the first equation might be

$$\langle 1 + w, 1 + 2w \rangle \quad \text{for any } w.$$

This solution is a generalization of our earlier solution $\langle 1, 1 \rangle$. The problem is now to find a special case of the general solution that also solves the second equation. In other words, we must find a w such that

$$2(1 + 2w) = (1 + w) + 2.$$

This strategy leads us to a solution.

Of course, the method of generalization does not apply to all conjunctive-goal problems. For instance, the synthesis of an integer square-root program has specifications

> Find z such that
> z is an integer and
> $z^2 \leqslant x$ and
> $(z + 1)^2 > x$,
> where $x \geqslant 0$.

The above approach of finding a general solution to one of the conjuncts and plugging it into the others is not effective in this case.

2.6. Side Effects

Up to now we have been considering programs in a LISP-like language: these programs return a value but effect no change in any data structure. In the next two sections we will consider the synthesis of programs with "side effects" that may modify the state of the world.

For instance, a LISP-like program to sort two variables x and y would return as its value a list of two numbers, either $(x\ y)$ or $(y\ x)$, without altering the contents of x and y. On the other hand, a program with side effects to sort x and y might change the contents of x and y.

In order to indicate that a program with side effects is to be constructed, we provide a specification of form

> Achieve P.

This construct means that the world is to be changed so as to make P true. For instance, if we specify a program

> Achieve $x = y$.

we intend that the program actually change the value of x or y, say by an assignment statement. However, if we specify

> Find x such that $x = y$,

the program constructed would return the value of y, but would not change the value of x or y.

Many of the techniques we used in the synthesis of LISP-like programs also apply to the construction of programs with side effects. In particular, we can use pattern-directed function invocation to retrieve tactical knowledge. The synthesis of the program in the following example has the same flavor as our earlier union example, but involves the introduction of side effects.

The program $sort(x\ y)$ to be constructed is to sort the values of two variables x and y. For simplicity we will allow the use of the statement $interchange(x\ y)$ to exchange the values of x and y, instead of the usual sequence of assignment statements. Our specification will be simply

$$\text{Achieve } x \leqslant y.$$

Strictly speaking, we should include in the specification the additional requirement that the set of values of x and y after the sort should be the same as before. However, we will not consider such compound goals until Section 2.8, and we can achieve the same effect by requiring that the *interchange* statement be the only instruction with side effects that appears in the program.

The first step in achieving a goal is to see if it is already true. (If a goal is a theorem, for instance, we do not need to construct a program to achieve it.) We cannot prove $x \leqslant y$, but we can use it as a basis for a hypothetical world split. This split corresponds to a conditional expression in the program being constructed. In flowchart notation the conditional expression is written as a program branch:

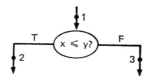

At point 2 our goal is already achieved. At point 3 we know that $\sim(x \leqslant y)$, i.e., $x > y$. To achieve $x \leqslant y$, it suffices to establish $x < y$, but this may be achieved by executing $interchange(x\ y)$. Thus we have $x \leqslant y$ in both worlds, and the final program is therefore:

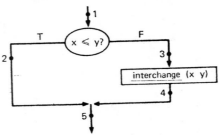

This example introduced no difficulties that our LISP-like program synthesis techniques could not handle. However, in general, programs with side effects must be given special treatment because of the necessity for representing changes in the world. It is important to be able to determine whether a given assertion is always true at a given point in a program. To this end we study the relationship between assertions and program constructs in the next section.

2.7. Assertions and Program Constructs

Suppose a program contains an assignment statement

and we wish to determine if $x \leqslant 3$ at Point 2. In order to do this it suffices to check if what we know at Point 1 implies that $y \leqslant 3$. In general, to determine an assertion of form $P(x)$ at Point 2, check $P(y)$ at Point 1. We will say that the assertion $P(y)$ is the result of "passing back" the assertion $P(x)$ from Point 2 to Point 1. [This is precisely the process outlined by Floyd (1967) and Hoare (1969).]

Furthermore, if our program contains the instruction

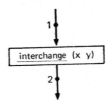

and we wish to establish $x \leqslant y$ at Point 2 we must check if $y \leqslant x$ at Point 1. In general, an assertion of form $P(x\ y)$ results in an assertion of form $P(y\ x)$ when passed back over *interchange*$(x\ y)$.

Suppose the program being constructed contains a branch

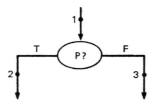

To determine if an assertion Q is true at Point 2, it suffices to check whether

$$Q \quad \text{if} \quad P$$

(i.e., $P \supset Q$) is true at Point 1. In order to determine if R is true at Point 3, it suffices to check whether

$$R \quad \text{if} \quad {\sim}P$$

(i.e., ${\sim}P \supset R$) is true at Point 1.

Suppose two control paths join in the program being constructed:

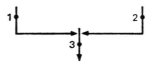

Thus to determine if assertion P is true at Point 3, it is sufficient to check that P be true at both Point 1 and Point 2.

Assertions may be passed back over complex programs. For instance, let us pass the assertion $y \leqslant z$ back over the program *sort*$(x\ y)$ which we constructed in the previous section. (See Figure 3.1.) By combining the methods that we have just introduced for passing assertions back over program constructs, we can see that in order to establish $y \leqslant z$ at Point 5, it is necessary to check that ($y \leqslant z$ if $x \leqslant y$) and ($x \leqslant z$ if ${\sim}(x \leqslant y)$) are true at Point 1.

Often the specification of a program will require the simultaneous satisfaction of more than one goal. As in the case of conjunctive goals in LISP-like programs, the special interest of this problem lies in

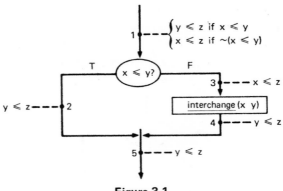

Figure 3.1.

the interrelatedness of the goals. The techniques of this section will now be applied to handle the interaction between goals.

2.8. Simultaneous Goals

A simultaneous-goal problem has the form

Achieve P and Q.

Sometimes P and Q will be independent conditions, so that we can achieve P and Q simply by achieving P and then achieving Q. For example, if our goal is

Achieve $x = 2$ and $y = 3$,

the two goals $x = 2$ and $y = 3$ are completely independent. In this section, however, we will be concerned with the more complex case in which P and Q interact. In such a case we may make P false in the course of achieving Q.

Consider for example the problem of sorting three variables x, y, and z. We will assume that the only instruction we can use is the subroutine $sort(u\ v)$, described in the previous section, which sorts two variables. Our goal is then

Achieve $x \leqslant y$ and $y \leqslant z$.

We know that the program $sort(u\ v)$ will achieve a goal of form $u \leqslant$

v. If we apply the straightforward technique of achieving the conjunct $x \leqslant y$ first, and then the conjunct $y \leqslant z$, we obtain the program

$$sort(x\ y)$$
$$sort(y\ z).$$

However, this program has a bug in that sorting y and z may disrupt the relation $x \leqslant y$: if z is initially the smallest of the three, in interchanging y and z we make y less than x. Reversing the order in which the conjuncts are achieved does not solve the problem.

There are a number of ways in which this problem may be resolved. One of them involves the notion of program modification [cf. Sussman (1975)]. The general strategy is as follows: to achieve P and Q simultaneously, first write a program to achieve P; then modify that program to achieve Q as well. The essence of this strategy, then, lies in a technique of program modification.

Let us see how this strategy applies to the simple sort problem. The specification is

Achieve $x \leqslant y$ and $y \leqslant z$.

It is easy to achieve $x \leqslant y$; the program $sort(x\ y)$ will do that immediately. We must now modify the program $sort(x\ y)$ to achieve $y \leqslant z$ without disturbing the relation $x \leqslant y$ we have just achieved. In other words, we would like to "protect" the relation $x \leqslant y$. We have seen that simply achieving $y \leqslant z$ after achieving $x \leqslant y$ is impossible without disturbing the protected relation. Therefore we will pass the goal $y \leqslant z$ back to the beginning of the program $sort(x\ y)$ and try to achieve it there, where there are no protected relations.

We have seen in the previous section that the goal $y \leqslant z$ passed back before the program $sort(x\ y)$ results in two goals:

(i) $y \leqslant z$ if $x \leqslant y$, and
(ii) $x \leqslant z$ if $\sim(x \leqslant y)$.

Both of these goals must be achieved before applying $sort(x\ y)$. We can achieve (i) by applying $sort(y\ z)$. (This will achieve $y \leqslant z$ whether or not $x \leqslant y$.) Our program so far is thus

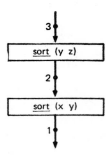

We still need to achieve goal (ii) at Point 2; we can achieve this goal simply by inserting the instruction *sort*(x z) before Point 2.

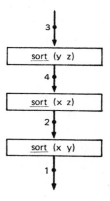

This modification will not effect Relation (i), "$y \leqslant z$ if $x \leqslant y$", which is protected at Point 2, because after executing *sort*(y z) and *sort*(x z), the value of z will be the largest of the three. Thus the desired program is

$$sort(y \ z)$$
$$sort(x \ z)$$
$$sort(x \ y).$$

If the subgoals are pursued in a different order, different variations on this program are obtained.

The program-modification strategy seems to be a fairly general approach to the simultaneous-goal problem. It also is a powerful program synthesis technique in general, as we will see when we develop the unification algorithm in Section 4.

This concludes the presentation of our basic program synthesis techniques. In the next part we will show how these same techniques work together in the synthesis of a more complex example.

3. Program Synthesis: The Pattern Matcher

We will present the synthesis of a simple pattern matcher to show how the concepts discussed in the previous section can be applied to a nontrivial problem. Later, in Section 4, we shall show how we can construct a more complex program, the unification algorithm of Robinson (1965), by modifying the pattern-matching program we are about to synthesize. We must first describe the data structures and primitive operations involved in the pattern matching and unification problems.

3.1. Domain and Notation

The main objects in our domain are *expressions* and *substitutions*.

3.1.1. Expressions

Expressions are atoms or nested lists of atoms; e.g., $(A\ B\ (X\ C)\ D)$ is an expression. An *atom* may be either a *variable* or a *constant*. (In our examples we will use $A, B, C, \ldots$ for constants and $U, V, W, \ldots$ for variables.) We have basic predicates *atom*, *var*, and *const* to distinguish these objects:

$$atom(l) \equiv l \text{ is an atom,}$$
$$var(l) \equiv l \text{ is a variable,}$$
$$const(l) \equiv l \text{ is a constant.}$$

To decompose an expression, we will use the primitive functions $head(l)$ and $tail(l)$, defined when l is not an atom.

$head(l)$ is the first element of l.
$tail(l)$ is the list of all but the first element of l.

Thus

$$head(((A\ (X)\ B)\ C\ (D\ X))) = (A\ (X)\ B),$$
$$tail(((A\ (X)\ B)\ C\ (D\ X))) = (C\ (D\ X)).$$

We will abbreviate $head(l)$ as l_h and $tail(l)$ as l_t.

To construct expressions we have the "$\cdot$" function: if l is any expression and m is a nonatomic expression, $l \cdot m$ is the expression formed by inserting l before the first element of m. For example,

$$A \cdot (B\ C\ D) = (A\ B\ C\ D),$$
$$(A\ (X)\ B) \cdot (C\ (D\ X)) = ((A\ (X)\ B)\ C\ (D\ X)).$$

The predicate $occursin(x\ l)$ is true if x is an atom that occurs in expression l at any level, e.g.,

$$occursin(A\ (C\ (B\ (A)\ B)\ C))\ \text{is true,}$$

but

$$occursin(X\ Y)\ \text{is false.}$$

Finally, we will introduce the predicate $constexp(l)$, which is true if l is made up entirely of constants. Thus

$$constexp((A\ (B)\ C\ (D\ E)))\ \text{is true.}$$

but

$$constexp(X)\ \text{is false.}$$

Note that $constexp$ differs from $const$ in that $constexp$ may be true for nonatomic expressions.

3.1.2. Substitutions

A substitution replaces certain variables of an expression by other expressions. We will represent a substitution as a list of pairs. Thus

$$(\langle X\ (A\ B)\rangle\ \langle Y\ (C\ Y)\rangle)$$

is a substitution.

The instantiation function $inst(s\ l)$ applies the substitution s to the expression l. For example, if

$$s = (\langle X\ (A\ B)\rangle\ \langle Y\ (C\ Y)\rangle)\ \text{ and }\ l = (X\ (A\ Y)\ X),$$

then

$$inst(s\ l) = ((A\ B)\ (A\ (C\ Y))\ (A\ B)).$$

Note that the substitution is applied by first replacing all occurrences of X simultaneously by $(A\ B)$ and then all occurrences of Y simultaneously by $(C\ Y)$. Thus, if

$$s' = (\langle X\ Y\rangle\ \langle Y\ C\rangle),$$

then

$$inst(s'\ l) = (C\ (A\ C)\ C).$$

The empty substitution Λ is represented by the empty list of pairs. Thus for any expression l,

$$inst(\Lambda\ l) = l.$$

We regard two substitutions s_1 and s_2 as equal (written $s_1 = s_2$) if and only if

$$inst(s_1\ l) = inst(s_2\ l)$$

for every expression l. Thus

$$(\langle X\ Y\rangle\ \langle Y\ C\rangle)\ \text{ and }\ (\langle X\ C\rangle\ \langle Y\ C\rangle)$$

are regarded as equal substitutions.

We can build up substitutions by using the functions *pair* and $\circ$ (composition): If v is a variable and t an expression, $pair(v\ t)$ is the substitution that replaces v by t; i.e.,

$$pair\,(v\ t) = (\langle v\ t\rangle).$$

If s_1 and s_2 are two substitutions, $s_1 \circ s_2$ is the substitution with the same effect as applying s_1 followed by s_2. Thus

$$inst(s_1 \circ s_2\ l) = inst(s_2\ inst(s_1\ l)).$$

For example if

$$s_1 = (\langle X\ A\rangle\ \langle Y\ B\ \rangle)\ \text{ and }\ s_2 = (\langle Z\ C\rangle\ \langle X\ D\rangle),$$

then

$$s_1 \circ s_2 = (\langle X\ A\rangle\ \langle Y\ B\rangle\ \langle Z\ C\rangle).$$

Note that for the empty substitution Λ,

$$\Lambda \circ s = s \circ \Lambda = s$$

for any substitution s.

3.2. The Specifications

The problem of pattern matching may be described as follows. We are given two expressions, *pat* and *arg*. While *pat* can be any expression, *arg* is assumed to contain no variables; i.e., *constexp(arg)* is true. We want to find a substitution z that transforms *pat* into *arg*, i.e., such that

$$inst(z \ pat) = arg.$$

We will call such a substitution a *match*. If no match exists, we want the program to return the distinguished constant NOMATCH. For example, if

$$pat \text{ is } (X \ A \ (Y \ B)) \text{ and } arg \text{ is } (C \ A \ (D \ B)),$$

we want the program to find the match

$$(\langle X \ C \rangle \langle Y \ D \rangle).$$

On the other hand, if

$$pat \text{ is } (X \ A \ (X \ B)) \text{ and } arg \text{ is } (B \ A \ (D \ B)),$$

then no substitution will transform *pat* into *arg*, because X cannot be matched with both B and D. Therefore the program should yield NOMATCH. (This version of the pattern matcher is simpler than the pattern matching algorithms usually implemented in programming languages because of the absence of "sequence" or "fragment" variables. Our variables must match exactly one expression, whereas a fragment variable may match any number of expressions.)

In mathematical notation the specifications for our pattern matcher are:

Goal 1. *match(pat arg)* = Find z such that *inst(z pat)* = *arg*
                  else z = NOMATCH,

where "Find z such that $P(z)$ else $Q(z)$" means construct an output z satisfying $P(z)$ if one exists; otherwise, find a z such that $Q(z)$.

The above specifications do not completely capture our intentions; for instance, if

$$pat \text{ is } (X \ Y) \text{ and } arg \text{ is } (A \ B),$$

then the substitution

$$z = (\langle X \ A \rangle \langle Y \ B \rangle \langle Z \ C \rangle)$$

will satisfy our specifications as well as

$$z = (\langle X \ A \rangle \langle Y \ B \rangle).$$

We have neglected to include in our specifications that no substitutions should be made for variables that do not occur in *pat*. We will call a match that satisfies this additional condition a *most general match*.

An interesting characteristic of the synthesis we present is that even if the user does not require that the match found be most general, the system will strengthen the specifications automatically to imply this condition, using the method outlined in Section 2.4. Therefore we will begin the synthesis using the weaker specifications.

3.3. The Base Cases

Rather than list all the knowledge we require in a special section at the beginning, we will mention a rule only when it is about to be used. Furthermore, if a rule seems excessively trivial we will omit it entirely. The general strategy is to first work on

Goal 2. Find z such that $inst(z \; pat) = arg$.

If this is found to be impossible (i.e., if it is *proven* that no such z exists), we will work on

Goal 3. Find a z such that z = NOMATCH;

which is seen to be trivially satisfied by taking z to be NOMATCH.

Thus, from now on we will be working primarily on Goal 2. However, in working on any goal we devote a portion of our time to showing that the goal is impossible to achieve. When we find cases in which Goal 2 is proven impossible, we will automatically return NOMATCH, which satisfies Goal 3.

We have in our knowledge base a number of rules concerning *inst,* including

Rule 1. $inst(s \; x) = x$ for any substitution s if $constexp(x)$
Rule 2. $inst(pair(v \; t) \; v) = t$ if $var(v)$.

We assume that these rules are retrieved by pattern-directed function invocation on Goal 2. Rule 1 can be applied only in the case that $constexp(pat)$ and $pat = arg$. We cannot prove either of these conditions; their truth or falsehood depends on the particular inputs to the program. We use these predicates as conditions for a hypothetical world split. In the case that both of these conditions are true, Rule 1 tells us that *any* substitution is a satisfactory match. We will have occasion to tighten the specifications of our program later; as they stand now, we will simply return "any", so as not to restrict our choice. The portion of the program we have constructed so far reads

$$match(pat\ arg) =$$
$$\text{if } constexp(pat)$$
$$\text{then if } pat = arg$$
$$\text{then any}$$
$$\text{else } \dots .$$

On the other hand, in the case $constexp(pat)$ and $pat \neq arg$, Rule 1 tells us that

$$inst(z\ pat) = pat \neq arg$$

for any z. Hence we are led to satisfy Goal 3 by returning NOMATCH.

We now consider the case

$$\sim constexp(pat).$$

Rule 2 establishes the subgoal

$$var(pat).$$

This is another occasion for a hypothetical world split. When $var(pat)$ is true, the program must return $pair(pat\ arg)$; the program we have constructed so far is

$$match(pat\ arg) =$$
$$\text{if } constexp(pat)$$
$$\text{then if } pat = arg$$
$$\text{then any}$$
$$\text{else NOMATCH}$$
$$\text{else if } var(pat)$$
$$\text{then } pair(pat\ arg)$$
$$\text{else } \dots .$$

Hencefore we assume $\sim var(pat)$. Recall that we have been assuming also that $\sim constexp(pat)$. To proceed we make use of the following additional knowledge about the function *inst*:

Rule 3. $inst(s \quad x \cdot y) = inst(s \quad x) \cdot inst(s \quad y)$
　　　　for any substitution s.

This rule applies to our Goal 2 if $pat = x \cdot y$ for some expressions x and y. We have some additional knowledge about expressions in general:

Rule 4. $u = u_h \cdot u_t$　if $\sim atom(u)$.

Recall that u_h is an abbreviation for $head(u)$ and u_t is an abbreviation for $tail(u)$.

Rule 5. $u \neq v \cdot w$　for any v and w if $atom(u)$.

Using Rule 4, we generate a subgoal

$$\sim atom(pat).$$

Since we have already assumed $\sim constexp(pat)$ and $\sim var(pat)$, we can actually prove $\sim atom(pat)$ using knowledge in the system. Therefore $pat = pat_h \cdot pat_t$, and using Rule 3 our Goal 2 is then reduced to

Goal 4. Find z such that $inst(z \quad pat_h) \cdot inst(z \quad pat_t) = $ arg.

We now make use of some general list-processing knowledge.

Rule 6. To prove $x \cdot y = u \cdot v$,　prove $x = u$ and $y = v$.

Applying this rule, we generate a subgoal to show that

$$arg = u \cdot v$$

for some u and v. Applying Rule 4, we know this is true with $u = arg_h$ and $v = arg_t$ if

$$\sim atom(arg).$$

This is another occasion for a hypothetical world split.

Thus, by Rule 6, in the case that $\sim atom(arg)$, our subgoal reduces to

Goal 5. Find z such that

$$inst(z\ pat_h) = arg_h$$

and

$$inst(z\ pat_t) = arg_t.$$

We will postpone treatment of this goal until after we have considered the other case, in which

$$atom(arg)$$

holds. In this case Rule 5 tells us that

$$inst(z\ pat_h)\cdot inst(z\ pat_t) \neq arg$$

for any z. Hence, our goal is unachievable in this case, and we can return NOMATCH.

The program so far is

$$match(pat\ arg) =$$
$$\text{if } constexp(pat)$$
$$\text{then if } pat = arg$$
$$\text{then any}$$
$$\text{else NOMATCH}$$
$$\text{else if } var(pat)$$
$$\text{then } pair(pat\ arg)$$
$$\text{else if } atom(arg)$$
$$\text{then NOMATCH}$$
$$\text{else... .}$$

For the as yet untreated case neither *pat* nor *arg* is atomic. Henceforth using Rule 4 we assume that *pat* is $pat_h\cdot pat_t$ and *arg* is $arg_h\cdot arg_t$.

3.4. The Inductive Case

We will describe the remainder of the synthesis in less detail, because the reader has already seen the style of reasoning we have been using. Recall that we had postponed our discussion of Goal 5 in order to consider the case in which *arg* is atomic. Now that we have completed our development of that case, we resume our work on Goal 5:

Find z such that $inst(z\ pat_h) = arg_h$ and $inst(z\ pat_t) = arg_t$.

This is a conjunctive goal, and is treated analogously to the goal in the simultaneous-linear-equations example (Section 2.5): The system will attempt to solve the first conjunct, using a recursive call to the pattern-matcher itself.

The interaction between the two conjuncts is part of the challenge of this synthesis. It is quite possible to satisfy each conjunct separately without being able to satisfy them both together. For example, if $pat = (X\ X)$ and $arg = (A\ B)$, then $pat_h = X$, $pat_t = (X)$, $arg_h = A$, and $arg_t = (B)$. Thus $z = (\langle X\ A\rangle)$ satisfies the first conjunct, $z = (\langle X\ B\rangle)$ satisfies the second conjunct, but no substitution will satisfy both conjuncts, because no substitution can match X against both A and B. Some mechanism is needed to ensure that the expression assigned to a variable in solving the first conjunct is the same as the expression assigned to that variable in solving the second conjunct.

There are several ways to approach this difficulty. For instance, the programmer may satisfy the two conjuncts separately and then attempt to combine the two substitutions thereby derived into a single substitution. Or he may actually replace those variables in pat_t that also occur in pat_h by whatever expressions they have been matched against, before attempting to match pat_t against arg_t. Or he may simply pass the substitution that satisfied the first conjunct as a third argument to the pattern matcher in working on the second conjunct. The pattern matcher must then check that the matches assigned to variables are consistent with the substitution given as the third argument.

We will examine in this section how a system would discover the second of these methods. A similar system could also discover the third method. We will not consider the first method here because it is not easily adapted to the unification problem.

Our strategy for approaching the conjunctive goal is as follows. We will consider the first conjunct independently:

Goal 6. Find z such that $inst(z\ pat_h) = arg_h$.

If we find a z that satisfies this goal, we will substitute that z into the second conjunct, giving

Goal 7. Prove $inst(z \ pat_t) = arg_t$.

If we are successful in Goal 7, we are done; however, if we fail, we will try to generalize z. In other words, we will try to find a broader class of substitutions that satisfy Goal 6 and from these select one that also satisfies Goal 7. This is the method we introduced to solve conjunctive goals in Section 2.5.

Applying this strategy, we begin work on Goal 6. We first use a rule that relates the construct

$$\text{Find } z \text{ such that } P(z)$$

to the construct

$$\text{Find } z \text{ such that } P(z) \text{ else } Q(z).$$

Rule 7. To find z such that $P(z)$, it suffices to find z_1 such that $P(z_1)$ else $Q(z_1)$, and $\sim Q(z_1)$ for some predicate Q.

This rule, applied to Goal 6, causes the generation of the subgoal

Goal 8. Find z_1 such that $inst(z_1 \ pat_h) = arg_h$ else $Q(z_1)$, and $\sim Q(z_1)$.

The first conjunct of this subgoal matches the top-level Goal 1, where $Q(z_1)$ is $z_1 = $ NOMATCH. This suggests establishing a recursion at this point, taking

$$z_1 = match(pat_h \ arg_h).$$

Henceforth we will use z_1 as an abbreviation for $match(pat_h \ arg_h)$. Termination is easily shown, because both pat_h and arg_h are proper subexpressions of *pat* and *arg*, respectively. It remains to show, according to Rule 7, that $z_1 \neq $ NOMATCH. This causes another hypothetical world split: in the case $z_1 = $ NOMATCH (i.e., no substitution can cause pat_h and arg_h to match), we can show that no substitution can cause *pat* and *arg* to match either, and hence can take $z = $ NOMATCH.

We have thus constructed the following new program segment

$$z_1 \leftarrow match(pat_h \; arg_h)$$
$$\text{if } z_1 = \text{NOMATCH}$$
$$\text{then NOMATCH}$$
$$\text{else}\ldots$$

We have used z_1 as a program variable to improve readability. The actual program constructed would use $match(pat_h \; arg_h)$ itself in place of z_1.

On the other hand, if $z_1 \neq \text{NOMATCH}$, we know that z_1 satisfies the first conjunct (Goal 6). Thus, in keeping with the conjunctive goal strategy, we try to show that z_1 satisfies the second conjunct (Goal 7) as well, i.e.,

$$inst(z_1 \; pat_t) = arg_t.$$

However, we fail in this attempt; in fact we can find sample inputs *pat* and *arg* that provide a counterexample to Goal 7 [e.g., *pat* = $(A \; X)$, *arg* = $(A \; B)$, $z_1 = \Lambda$]. Thus we go back and try to generalize our solution to Goal 6.

We already have a solution to Goal 6: we know $inst(z_1 \; pat_h) = arg_h$. We also can deduce that $constexp(arg_h)$, because we have assumed $constexp(arg)$. Hence Rule 1 tells us that

$$inst(z_2 \; arg_h) = arg_h$$

for any substitution z_2. Therefore

$$inst(z_2 \; inst(z_1 \; pat_h)) = arg_h,$$

i.e.,

$$inst(z_1 \circ z_2 \quad pat_h) = arg_h$$

for any substitution z_2. Thus having one substitution z_1 that satisfies Goal 6, we have an entire class of substitutions, of form $z_1 \circ z_2$, each of which satisfies Goal 6. These substitutions may be considered to be "extensions" of z_1; although z_1 itself may not satisfy Goal 7, perhaps some extension of z_1 will.

The above reasoning is straightforward enough to justify, but further work is needed to motivate a machine to pursue it.

It remains now to find a single z_2 such that $z_1 \circ z_2$ satisfies Goal

7, i.e.,

Goal 9. Find z_1 such that $inst(z_1 \circ z_2 \ pat_t) = arg_t$, or equivalently,
               Find z_2 such that $inst(z_2 \ inst(z_1 \ pat_t)) = arg_t$.
Applying Rule 7, we establish a new goal:

Goal 10. Find z_2 such that $inst(z_2 \ inst(z_1 \ pat_t)) = arg_t$ else $Q(z_2)$,
               and $\sim Q(z_2)$.

The first conjunct of this goal is an instance of our top-level goal,
taking *pat* to be $inst(z_1 \ pat_t)$, *arg* to be arg_t, and $Q(z_2)$ to be $z_2 =$
NOMATCH. Thus we attempt to insert the recursive call

$$z_2 \leftarrow match(inst(z_1 \ pat_t) \ arg_t)$$

into our program at this point. (Again, the introduction of z_2 as a
program variable is for notational simplicity.) However, we must
first establish

$$\sim Q(z_2),$$

i.e.,

$$z_2 \neq \text{NOMATCH}.$$

We cannot prove this: it is true for some examples and false for
others. Therefore we split on this condition.
   In the case $z_2 \neq$ NOMATCH Goal 10 is satisfied. Thus z_2 also
satisfies Goal 9, and $z = z_1 \circ z_2$ satisfies Goal 7.
   Our program so far is

$$match(pat \ arg) =$$
               if $constexp(pat)$
               then if $pat = arg$
                       then any
                       else NOMATCH
               else if $var(pat)$
                       then $pair(pat \ arg)$
                       else if $atom(arg)$
                               then NOMATCH
                               else $z_1 \leftarrow match(pat_h \ arg_h)$
                                       if $z_1 = $ NOMATCH

then NOMATCH
else $z_2 \leftarrow match(inst(z_1 \; pat_t) \; arg_t)$
    if z_2 = NOMATCH
    then. . .
    else $z_1 \circ z_2$.

3.5. The Strengthening of the Specifications

We have gone this far through the synthesis using the weak specifications, i.e., without requiring that the match found be most general. In fact, the match found may or may not be most general, depending on the value taken for the unspecified substitution "any" produced in the very first case. The synthesis is nearly complete. However, we will be unable to continue it without strengthening the specifications and modifying the program accordingly. We now have only one case left to consider. This is the case in which

$$z_2 = \text{NOMATCH},$$

i.e.,

$$match(inst(z_1 \; pat_t) \; arg_t) = \text{NOMATCH}.$$

This means that no substitution w satisfies

$$inst(w \; inst(z_1 \; pat_t)) = arg_t,$$

or, equivalently,

$$inst(z_1 \circ w \quad pat_t) \neq arg_t \quad \text{for every substitution } w.$$

This means that no substitution of form $z_1 \circ w$ could possibly satisfy

$$inst(z_1 \circ w \quad pat) = arg.$$

We here have a choice: we can try to find a substitution s not of form $z_1 \circ w$ that satisfies.

$$inst(s \; pat_h) = arg_h$$

and repeat the process; or we could try to show that only a substitution s of form $z_1 \circ w$ could possibly satisfy

$$inst(s \; pat_h) = arg_h,$$

and therefore we take z = NOMATCH.

Pursuing the latter course, we try to show that the set of substitutions s of form $z_1 \circ w$ is the entire set of solutions to

$$inst(s\ pat_h) = arg_h.$$

In other words, we show that for any substitution s,

$$\text{if } inst(s\ pat_h) = arg_h \quad \text{then } s = z_1 \circ w \text{ for some } w.$$

This condition is equivalent to saying that z_1 is a most general match. We cannot prove this about z_1 itself; however, since z_1 is $match(pat_h\ arg_h)$, it suffices to add the condition to the specifications for $match$, as described in Section 2.4. The strengthened specifications now read

$$
\begin{aligned}
&\text{Find } z \text{ such that} \\
&\{inst(z\ pat) = arg \text{ and} \\
&\text{for all } s\ [\text{if } inst(s\ pat) = arg \\
&\qquad\qquad \text{then } s = z \circ w \text{ for some } w]\} \\
&\text{else } z = \text{NOMATCH.}
\end{aligned}
$$

Once we have strengthened the specifications it is necessary to go through the entire program and see that the new, stronger specifications are satisfied, modifying the program if necessary. In this case no major modifications are necessary; however, the assignment

$$z \leftarrow any$$

that occurs in the case in which pat and arg are equal and constant is further specified to read

$$z \leftarrow \Lambda.$$

Our final program is therefore

$$
\begin{aligned}
&match(pat\ arg) = \\
&\quad \text{if } constexp(pat) \\
&\quad \text{then if } pat = arg \\
&\qquad\quad \text{then } \Lambda \\
&\qquad\quad \text{else NOMATCH} \\
&\quad \text{else if } var(pat) \\
&\qquad\quad \text{then } pair(pat\ arg) \\
&\qquad\quad \text{else if } atom(arg) \\
&\qquad\qquad\quad \text{then NOMATCH} \\
&\qquad\qquad\quad \text{else } z_1 \leftarrow match(pat_h\ arg_h) \\
&\qquad\qquad\qquad \text{if } z_1 = \text{NOMATCH}
\end{aligned}
$$

$$\text{then NOMATCH}$$
$$\text{else } z_2 \leftarrow match(inst(z_1 \ pat_t) \ arg_t)$$
$$\text{if } z_2 = \text{NOMATCH}$$
$$\text{then NOMATCH}$$
$$\text{else } z_1 \circ z_2 .$$

The above pattern matcher is only one of many pattern-matchers that can be derived to satisfy the same specifications. In pursuing the synthesis the system has made many choices; some of the alternative paths result in a failure to solve the problem altogether, whereas other paths result in different, possibly better programs.

4. Program Modification: The Unification Algorithm

In general, we cannot expect a system to synthesize an entire complex program from scratch, as in the pattern-matcher example. We would like the system to remember a large body of programs that have been synthesized before, and the method by which they were constructed. When presented with a new problem, the system should check to see if it has solved a similar problem before. If so, it may be able to adapt the technique of the old program to make it solve the new problem.

There are several difficulties involved in this approach. First, we cannot expect the system to remember every detail of every synthesis in its history. Therefore, it must decide what to remember and what to forget. Second, the system must decide which problems are similar to the one being considered, and the concept of similarity is somewhat ill defined. Third, having found a similar program, the system must somehow modify the old synthesis to solve the new problem. We will concentrate only on the last of these problems in this discussion. We will illustrate a technique for program modification as applied to the synthesis of a version of Robinson's unification algorithm (1965).

4.1. The Specifications

Unification may be considered to be a generalization of pattern-matching in which variables appear in both *pat* and *arg*. The problem is to find a single substitution (called a "unifier") that, when applied to both *pat* and *arg,* will yield identical expressions. For instance, if

$$pat = (X A)$$

and

$$arg = (B Y),$$

then a possible unifier of *pat* and *arg* is

$$(\langle X B \rangle \langle Y A \rangle).$$

The close analogy between pattern-matching and unification is clear. If we assume that the system remembers the pattern-matcher we constructed in Sections 3.2 through 3.5 and the goal structure involved in the synthesis, the solution to the unification problem is greatly facilitated.

The specifications for the unification algorithm, in mathematical notation, are

> *unify*(*pat arg*) =
> Find z such that *inst*(z *pat*) = *inst*(z *arg*)
> else z = NOUNIFY.

4.2. The Analogy with the Pattern Matcher

For purpose of comparison we rewrite the *match* specifications:

> *match*(*pat arg*) =
> Find z such that *inst*(z *pat*) = *arg*
> else z = NOMATCH.

In formulating the analogy, we identify *unify* with *match, pat* with *pat,* the *arg* in *unify*(*pat arg*) with *arg, inst*(z *arg*) also with *arg,* and NOMATCH with NOUNIFY. In accordance with this analogy, we must systematically alter the goal structure of the pattern-matcher synthesis. For example, Goal 5 becomes modified to read

$$\text{Find } z \text{ such that } inst(z \; pat_h) = inst(z \; arg_h)$$
$$\text{and } inst(z \; pat_t) = inst \; (z \; arg_t).$$

In constructing the pattern matcher, we had to break down the synthesis into various cases. We will try to maintain this case structure in formulating our new program. Much of the saving derived from modifying the pattern matcher instead of constructing the unification algorithm from scratch arises because we do not have to deduce the case splitting all over again.

A difficult step in the pattern matcher synthesis involved the strengthening of the specifications for the entire program. We added the condition that the match found was to be "most general". In formulating the unification synthesis, we will immediately strengthen the specifications in the analogous way. The strengthened specifications read

$$unify(pat\ arg) =$$
$$\text{Find } z \text{ such that}$$
$$\{\ inst(z\ pat) = inst(z\ arg) \text{ and}$$
$$\text{for all } s\ [\text{if } inst(s\ pat) = inst(s\ arg)$$
$$\text{then } s = z \circ w \text{ for some } w\ ]\}$$
$$\text{else } z = \text{NOUNIFY}.$$

Following Robinson, we will refer to a unifier satisfying the new condition as a "most general unifier".

Note that this alteration process is purely syntactic; there is no reason to assume that the altered goal structure corresponds to a valid line of reasoning. For instance, the mere fact that achieving Goal 2 in the pattern-matching program is useful in achieving Goal 1 does not necessarily imply that achieving the corresponding Goal 2' in the unification algorithm will have any bearing on Goal 1'. The extent to which the reasoning carries over depends on the soundness of the analogy. If a portion of the altered goal structure proves to be valid, the corresponding segment of the program can remain; otherwise, we must construct a new program segment.

4.3. The Modification

Let us examine the first two cases of the unification synthesis in full detail, so that we can see exactly how the modification process works. In the pattern matcher, we generated the subgoal (Goal 2)

$$\text{Find } z \text{ such that } inst(z\ pat) = arg.$$

The corresponding unification subgoal is

$$\text{Find } z \text{ such that } inst(z\ pat) = inst(z\ arg).$$

In the pattern matcher we first considered the case *constexp(pat)* where *pat* = *arg*. In this case the corresponding program segment will return Λ. This segment also satisfies the modified goal in this case, because

$$inst(\Lambda\ pat) = inst(\Lambda\ arg).$$

The system must also check that Λ is a most general unifier, i.e.,

for all *s* [if *inst(s pat)* = *inst(s arg)*

then *s* = Λ ∘ *w* for some *w*].

This condition is easily satisfied, taking *w* = *s*. Thus, in this case, the program segment is correct without any modification.

The next case does require some modification. In the pattern matcher, when *constexp(pat)* is true and *pat* ≠ *arg*, *z* is taken to be NOMATCH. However, in this case in the unification algorithm we must check that

$$inst(s\ pat) \neq inst(s\ arg),$$

i.e.,

$$pat \neq inst(s\ arg)$$

for any *s*, in order to take *z* = NOUNIFY. Since for the unification problem *arg* may contain variables, this condition cannot be satisfied. We must therefore try to achieve the specifications in some other way. In this case [where *constexp(pat)*], the specifications of the unification algorithm reduce to

Find *z* such that

{*pat* = *inst(z arg)* and

for all *s* [if *pat* = *inst(s arg)*

then *s* = *z* ∘ *w* for some *w*]}

else *z* = NOUNIFY.

These specifications are precisely the specifications of the pattern matcher with *pat* and *arg* reversed; consequently, we can invoke *match(arg pat)* at this point in the program.

The balance of the modification can be carried out in the same manner. The derived unification algorithm is

unify(pat arg) =
    if *constexp(pat)*
    then if *pat* = *arg*
        then Λ
        else *match(arg pat)*

else if $var(pat)$
  then if $occursin(pat\ arg)$
  then NOUNIFY
  else $pair(pat\ arg)$
else if $atom(arg)$
  then $unify(arg\ pat)$
  else $z_1 \leftarrow unify(pat_h\ arg_h)$
    if z_1 = NOUNIFY
    then NOUNIFY
    else $z_2 \leftarrow unify(inst(z_1\ pat_t)\ inst(z_1\ arg_t))$
      if z_2 = NOUNIFY
      then NOUNIFY
      else $z_1 \circ z_2$.

Recall that $occursin(pat\ arg)$ means that pat occurs in arg as a sub-expression.

The termination of this program is considerably more difficult to prove than was the termination of the pattern matcher. However, the construction of the unification algorithm from the pattern matcher is much easier than the initial synthesis of the pattern matcher itself.

Note that the program we have constructed contains a redundant branch. The expression

if $pat = arg$
then Λ
else $match(arg\ pat)$

could be reduced to

$match(arg\ pat)$.

Such improvements would not be made until a later optimization phase.

5. Discussion

5.1. Implementation

Implementation of the techniques presented in this paper is under-way. Some of them have already been implemented. Others will require further development before an implementation will be possible.

We imagine the rules, used to represent reasoning tactics, to be expressed as programs in a PLANNER-type language. Our own implementation is in QLISP (Wilber, 1976). Rules are summoned by pattern-directed function invocation.

World splitting has been implemented using the *context* mechanism of QLISP, which was introduced in QA4 [Rulifson et al., (1972)]. Although the world splitting has been implemented, we have yet to experiment with the various strategies for controlling it.

The existing system is capable of producing simple programs such as the union function, the program to sort two variables from Section 2, or the loop-free segments of the pattern-matcher from Section 3.

The generalization of specifications (Section 2.4 and 3.5) is a difficult technique to apply without its going astray. We will develop heuristics to regulate it in the course of the implementation. Similarly, our approach to conjunctive goals (Section 2.5) needs further explication.

5.2. Historical Context and Contemporary Research

Early work in program synthesis [e.g., Simon (1963), Green (1969), Waldinger and Lee (1969)] was limited by the problem-solving capabilities of the respective formalisms involved (the General Problem Solver in the case of Simon; resolution-theorem-proving in the case of the others). Our paper on loop formation (Manna and Waldinger, 1971) was set in a theorem-proving framework, and paid little attention to the implementation problems.

It is typical of contemporary program synthesis work not to attempt to restrict itself to a formalism; systems are more likely to write programs the way a human programmer would write them. For example, the recent work of Sussman (1975) is modeled after the debugging process. Rather than trying to produce a correct program at once, Sussman's system rashly goes ahead and writes incorrect programs which it then proceeds to debug. The work reported in Green (1976) attempts to model a very experienced programmer. The system relies on built-in knowledge rather than on inference or problem solving ability.

The work reported here emphasizes reasoning more heavily than the papers of Sussman and Green. For instance, in our synthesis of the pattern matcher we assumed no knowledge about pattern matching itself. Of course we do assume extensive knowledge of lists, substitutions, and other aspects of the subject domain.

Although Sussman's debugging approach has influenced our treatment of program modification and the handling of simultaneous goals, we tend to rely more on logical methods than Sussman. Furthermore, Sussman deals only with programs that manipulate blocks on a table; therefore he has not been forced to deal with problems that are more crucial in conventional programming, such as the formation of conditionals and loops.

The work of Buchanan and Luckham (1974) is closest to ours in the problems it addresses. However, their system forms iterative loops that must be specified in advance by the user as "iterative rules", whereas in our system the loops are recursive and are introduced by the system itself when it recognizes a relationship between the top-level goal and a subgoal. Buchanan and Luckham's methods for forming conditionals and for treating programs with side effects are also somewhat different from ours.

5.3. Conclusion and Future Work

Some of the approaches to program synthesis that we feel will be most fruitful in the future have been given little emphasis in this paper because they are not yet fully developed. For example, the technique of program modification, which occupied only one small part of the current paper, we feel to be central to future program synthesis work. The retention of previously constructed programs is a powerful way to acquire and store knowledge. Furthermore, program optimization [cf. Darlington and Burstall (1973)] and program debugging are just special cases of program modification.

We hope we have managed to convey in this paper the promise of program synthesis, without giving the false impression that automatic synthesis is likely to be immediately practical. A computer system that can replace the human programmer will very likely have human intelligence in other respects as well.

Acknowledgments

We wish to thank Robert Boyer, Nachum Dershowitz, Bertram Raphael, and Georgia Sutherland for detailed critical readings of the manuscript. We would also like to thank Peter Deutsch, Richard Fikes, Akira Fusaoka, Cordell Green and his students, Irene Greif, Carl Hewitt, Shmuel Katz, David Luckham, Earl Sacerdoti, and Ben Wegbreit for conversations that aided in formulating the ideas in this paper. The set-theoretic expression-handler is based on work of Jan Derksen.

The research reported herein was sponsored by the National Science Foundation primarily under Grant GJ-36146 (SRI Project 2245) and partially under Grant GK-35493 (SRI Project 2323).

Postscript

Since the original appearance of the papers in this collection, much related research has been done. In this postscript we do not catalogue all the papers that have appeared on these topics, but we do mention some closely related work and some general trends.

Program Verification

Since the paper "Reasoning about Programs" was written, several more powerful verification systems have appeared using the same invariant-assertion technique. The system of Suzuki (1975), for example, can handle a wider class of programs and is significantly faster than the system we describe. Good et al. (1975), on the other hand, allow much more interaction between the user and the theorem prover. Much work has been done also in extending the technique to allow a wider class of data and control structures in the verified programs. At the same time, alternate techniques for program verification besides the invariant-assertion method have been proposed.

Analysis of Programs

Much work has also been done related to the topic of the second paper, "Logical Analysis of Programs." German and Wegbreit (1975) have implemented some heuristic approaches for generating invariant assertions. The counters approach to proving program termination has been incorporated into the program verification system of Luckham and Suzuki (1975). A system to analyze the running time of programs has been implemented by Wegbreit (1975). Efforts have been made to use such analyses as a basis for the optimization of programs and as a guide for their synthesis.

Program Synthesis

The recursion-introduction technique that appears in "Knowledge and Reasoning in Program Synthesis" has been further developed by Siklóssy (1974) and Darlington (1975). The simultaneous goal strategy has been elaborated on and implemented by Warren (1974) and Waldinger (1977). Other approaches to the automatic construction of computer programs are being pursued, under the general rubric of *automatic programming*. Most of these approaches are less formal than ours in specifying the program to be constructed, and less systematic in developing it. For a comprehensive survey of this field, see Biermann (1976).

References

Balzer, R. M. (Sept. 1972). *Automatic Programming.* Technical Report. Information Science Institute, University of Southern California, Marina del Rey, Ca.

Biermann, A. W. (1976). Approaches to automatic programming. In *Advances in Computers,* vol. 15. New York: Academic Press (to appear).

Biermann, A. W. and R. Krishnaswamy (Sept. 1976). Constructing programs from example computations. *IEEE Transactions on Software Engineering,* 2 (3): 141–153.

Boyer, R. S., and J S. Moore (Jan. 1975). Proving theorems about LISP functions. *JACM,* 22(1): 129–144.

Buchanan, J. R., and D. C. Luckham (May 1974). *On Automating the Construction of Programs.* Technical report. Artificial Intelligence Laboratory, Stanford University, Stanford, Ca..

Burstall, R. M., and J. Darlington (Jan. 1977). A transformation system for developing recursive programs, *JACM,* 24 (1): 44–67.

Cooper, D. C. (1971). Programs for mechanical program verification. In *Machine Intelligence* 6, New York: Elsevier North-Holland, pp. 43–59.

Darlington, J. (July 1975). Applications of program transformation to program synthesis. In *Colloques IRIA on Proving and Improving Programs.* Arc et Senans, France, pp. 133–144.

Darlington, J., and R. M. Burstall (Aug. 1973). A system which automatically improves programs. *In Proceedings of the Third International Joint Conference on Artificial Intelligence,* Stanford, Ca., pp. 479–485.

Deutsch, L. P. (June 1973). *An Interactive Program Verifier.* Ph.D. thesis. University of California, Berkeley, Ca.

Elspas, B., K. N. Levitt, and R. J. Waldinger (Sept. 1973). *An Interactive System for the Verification of Computer Programs.* Technical report. Stanford Research Institute, Menlo Park, Ca..

Elspas, B. (July 1974). *The Semiautomatic Generation of Inductive Assertions for Proving Program Correctness.* Technical report. Stanford Research Institute, Menlo Park, Ca.

Floyd, R. W. (1967). Assigning meanings to programs. In *Proceedings of the Symposium in Applied Mathematics,* vol. 19 (J. T. Schwartz, ed.), American Mathematical Society, Providence, R. I., pp. 19-32.

Floyd, R. W. (1971). Towards interactive design of correct programs. In *Proceedings of IFIP Congress,* vol. 1, Amsterdam: North-Holland, pp. 7-10.

German, S. M., and B. Wegbreit (Mar. 1975). Proving loop programs. *IEEE Transactions on Software Engineering,* 1 (1): 68-75.

Good, D. I., R. L. London, and W. W. Bledsoe (Mar. 1975). An interactive program verification system. *IEEE Transactions on Software Engineering,* 1 (1): 59-67.

Green, C. (May 1969). Application of theorem proving to problem solving, In *Proceedings of International Joint Conference on Artificial Intelligence,* Washington, D.C. pp. 219-239.

Green, C. (Oct. 1976). The design of PSI program synthesis system. In *Proceedings of Second International Conference on Software Engineering.* San Francisco, Ca., pp. 4-18.

Greif, I. and R. Waldinger (April 1974). A more mechanical heuristic approach to program verification. In *Proceedings of International Symposium on Programming,* Paris, pp. 83-90.

Hardy, S. (Sept. 1975). Synthesis of LISP programs from examples, In *Proceedings of the Fourth International Joint Conference on Artificial Intelligence,* Tbilisi, Georgia, USSR, pp. 240-245.

Hewitt, C. (April 1971). *Description and Theoretical Analysis (Using Schemata) of PLANNER: A Language for Proving Theorems and Manipulating Models in a Robot.* Ph.D. thesis M.I.T., Cambridge, Mass.

Hoare, C. A. R. (July 1961). Algorithm 65: FIND, *CACM,* 4 (7): 321.

Hoare, C. A. R. (Oct. 1969). An axiomatic basis of computer programming, *CACM,* 12 (10): 576-580, 583.

Hoare, C. A. R. (Jan. 1971). Proof of a program: FIND. *CACM,* 14 (1): 39-45.

Igarashi, S., R. L. London, and D. C. Luckham (1975). Automatic program verification I: A logical basis and its implementation. *Acta Informatica,* 4 (2): 145-182.

Katz, S. M., and Z. Manna (Aug. 1973). A heuristic approach to program verification. In *Proceedings of the Third International Conference on Artificial Intelligence,* Stanford University, Stanford, Ca., pp. 143-155.

Katz, S. M., and Z. Manna (1975). A closer look at termination. *Acta Informatica*, 5 (4): 333–352.

Katz, S. M., and Z. Manna (Apr. 1976). Logical analysis of programs. *CACM*, 19 (4): 188–206. (The second paper in this collection.)

King, J. C. (1969). *A Program Verifier.* Ph.D. thesis. Carnegie-Mellon University, Pittsburgh, Pa.

King, J. C. (1970). A verifying compiler. In *Debugging Techniques in Large Systems* (Randall Rustin, ed.), Englewood Cliffs, N.J.: Prentice-Hall, pp. 17–39.

Knuth, D. E. (1968). *The Art of Computer Programming, Volume 1: Fundamental Algorithms.* Reading, Mass: Addison-Wesley.

Knuth, D. E. (1969). *The Art of Computer Programming, Volume 2: Seminumerical Algorithms.* Reading, Mass: Addison-Wesley.

Kowlaski, R. (March 1974). *Logic for Problem Solving.* Technical report. University of Edinburgh, Edinburgh.

Luckham, D. C., and N. Suzuki (Oct. 1975). *Proof of Termination within a Weak Logic of Programs,* Technical report. Stanford University, Stanford, Ca.

Manna, Z. (May 1969). The correctness of programs. *JCSS*, 3 (2): 119–127.

Manna, Z. (1974). *Mathematical Theory of Computation.* New York: McGraw-Hill.

Manna, Z., and A. Pnueli (July 1970). Formalization of properties of functional programs. *JACM*, 17 (3): 555–569.

Manna, Z., and R. Waldinger (March 1971). Toward automatic program synthesis. *CACM*, 14 (3): 151–165.

Manna, Z., and R. Waldinger (1975). Knowledge and reasoning in program synthesis. *Artificial Intelligence*, 6 (2): 175–208. (The third paper in this collection.)

McCarthy, J. (1962). Towards a mathematical science of computation. In *Information Processing, Proceedings of IFIP Congress 1962* (C. M. Popplewell, ed.). Amsterdam: North-Holland, pp. 21–28.

McCarthy, J., P. W. Abrahams, D. J. Edwards, T. P. Hart, and M. I. Levin (Aug. 1962). *LISP 1.5 Programmer's Manual.* Cambridge, Mass.: M.I.T. Press,

Naur, P. (1966). Proof of algorithms by general snapshots. *BIT*, 6: 310–316.

Robinson, J. A. (Jan. 1965). A machine oriented logic based on the resolution principle. *JACM*, 12 (1): 23–41.

Rulifson, J. F., J. A. Derksen, and R. J. Waldinger (Nov. 1972). *QA4: A Procedural Calculus for Intuitive Reasoning.* Technical report. Stanford Research Institute, Menlo Park, Ca.

Siklóssy, L. (Nov. 1974). The synthesis of programs from their properties, and the insane heuristic. In *Proceedings of the Third Texas Conference on Computing Systems,* Austin, Texas.

Simon, H. A. (Oct. 1963). Experiments with a heuristic compiler. *JACM,* 10 (4): 493–506.

Sites, R. L. (May 1974). *Proving that Computer Programs Terminate Cleanly.* Ph.D. thesis. Stanford University, Stanford, Ca.

Summers, P. D. (Jan. 1976). A methodology for LISP program construction from examples. In *Proceedings of the Third ACM Symposium on Principles of Programming Languages,* Atlanta, Ga., pp. 68–76.

Sussman, G. J. (1975). *A Computer Model of Skill Acquisition.* New York: Elsevier North-Holland.

Suzuki, N. (Apr. 1975). Verifying programs by algebraic and logical reduction. In *Proceedings of the International Conference on Reliable Software,* Los Angeles, Ca., pp. 473–481.

Teitelman, W. (Dec. 1975). *INTERLISP Reference Manual,* Xerox PARC, Palo Alto, Ca.

Turing, A. M. (Jan. 1950). Checking a large routine. In *Report of a Conference on High Speed Automatic Calculating Machines,* University of Toronto, Canada, pp. 66–69.

von Neumann, J., and H. H. Goldstine (1963). Planning and coding problems for an electronic computer instrument, Part 2. In *Collected Works of John von Neumann.* vol. 5, New York: Macmillan, pp. 91–99.

Waldinger, R. J. (1977). Achieving several goals simultaneously. In *Machine Intelligence 8: Machine Representations of Knowledge* (E. W. Elcock and D. Michie, eds.). New York: John Wiley and Sons, Inc.

Waldinger, R. J., and R. C. T. Lee (May 1969). PROW: A step toward automatic program writing, In *Proceedings of International Joint Conference on Artificial Intelligence,* Washington, D.C., pp. 241–252.

Waldinger, R. J., and K. N. Levitt (1974). Reasoning about programs. *Artificial Intelligence,* 5: 235–316.(The first paper in this collection.)

Warren, D. H. D. (June 1976). Warplan: A System for Generating Plans. Memo. University of Edinburgh, Edinburgh, Scotland.

Wegbreit, B. (Feb. 1974). The synthesis of loop predicates. *CACM,* 17 (2): 163–167.

Wegbreit, B. (Sept. 1975). Mechanical program analysis. *CACM,* 18 (9): 528–539.

Wensley, J. H. (1958). A class of non-analytical interactive processes. *Computer Journal,* 1: 163–167.

Wilber, B. M. (March 1976). A QLISP Reference Manual. Technical report. Stanford Research Institute, Menlo Park, Ca.

Name Index

Abrahams, P.W., 15,22

Balzer, R.M., 143
Biermann, A.W., 142,180
Bledsoe, W.W., 93,179
Boyer, R.S., 1,147
Buchanan, J.R., 177
Burstall, R.M., 148,177,

Cooper, D.C., 139

Darlington, J., 148,177,180
Derksen, J.A.C., 2,38,176
Deutsch, L.P., 1,30,93

Edwards, D.J., 15,22
Elspas, B., 2,7,139

Floyd, R.W., 3,8,37,93,121,124,139,
    140,152

German, S.M., 7,179
Goldstine, H.H., 3
Good, D.I., 93,179
Green, C., 176,177
Greif, I., 139

Hardy, S., 142
Hart, T.P., 15,22
Hein, P., 1
Hewitt, C., 13,142,143
Hoare, C.A.R., 1,3,28,30,35,152

Igarashi, S., 1,30

Katz, S.M., 7,126,139
King, J.C., 1,19,35,36,93,139
Kowalski, R., 143
Knuth, D.E., 3,15,139
Krishnaswamy, R., 142

Lee, R.C.T., 176
Levin, M.I., 15 22
Levitt, K.N., 2,93,139
London, R.L., 1,30,93,179
Luckham, D.C., 1,30,177,179

Manna, Z., 7,25,96,119,126,139,146,
    176
McCarthy, J., 15,19,22
Moore, J.S., 1,147

Naur, P., 3
von Neumann, J., 3

Pnueli, A., 25

Reboh, R., 36
Robinson, J.A., 22,23,157,171
Rulifson, J.F., 2,38,176

Sacerdoti, E.D., 36
Siklossy, L., 180
Simon, H.A., 176
Sites, R.L., 139
Summers, P.D., 142

187

Sussman, G.J., 139,155,176,177
Suzuki, N., 93,179

Teitelman, W., 2
Turing, A.M., 3

Waldinger, R.J., 2,38,93,139,146,176,
    180
Warren, D.H.D., 180
Wegbreit, B., 7,139,179
Wensley, J.H., 20,21,74,105
Wilber, B.M., 36,142,176

Subject Index

access function, 19f, 55
adaptation (of programs). *See* modification.
addition function. *See* plus function.
ALGOL (programming language), 28ff
analogy (in program synthesis), 172ff
    and function, 16, 38
arrays, 18ff, 27ff, 55ff, 84ff
assertions, 3ff
    input, 3, 93ff
    intermediate, 6. *see also* invariants.
    output, 3, 93ff
    in QA4, 16ff, 41
assignment statements
    and synthesis, 150ff
    and verification, 4, 9, 101ff
associativity, 15, 53
automatic programming, 180

backtracking (in QA4), 12ff, 36ff, 38, 47
bags (in QA4), 15, 18, 45, 47, 62f
blocked programs, 95
blocks world, 177
bounding variables (invariant generation rule), 111f

cancelation, 53
case analysis. *See* hypothetical reasoning.
change function, 19f, 55, 58
commutativity, 15
complete set (of cutpoints), 96
composition function, 66, 159
conditional expressions, 46, 103ff
    formation of, 142, 144ff, 151ff, 177

conjunct elimination (invariant generation rule), 110
conjunction function. *See* and function.
conjunctive goals, 148ff, 165ff, 176. (*See also* simultaneous goals.)
construction (of programs). *See* synthesis.
contexts (in QA4), 17, 34f, 43, 48, 176
correctness of programs, 2ff, 93ff, 119ff
counter-examples (for incorrect programs), 37
counters (for proving termination), 95ff, 124ff, 139, 179
cutpoints (of loops), 95ff

data structures, 15ff, 179
debugging (of programs), 94, 123, 127ff, 139f, 176f
demon (in QA4), 14, 48ff
depth-first search, 36
development (of programs). *See* synthesis.
diagnosis (of programs). *See* debugging.
difference equations, 102
difference function (numerical). *See* minus function.
difference function (on bags), 58, 62f
disjunct elimination (invariant generation rule), 109
disjunction function. *See* or function.
distributive law, 52f
divide function, 12f, 47f, 53
division algorithm, integer (example), 20ff, 74ff, 105, 113ff, 122ff

division algorithm, real number (example), 105ff, 112f, 123ff

ellipsis notation, 6, 8ff, 143, 181
equal function, 1, 12ff, 16, 27, 36f, 39ff, 46f, 67ff
equality. *See* equal function.
equivalence relations, 15
Euclidean algorithm (example), 35
exchange sort (example), 36
exchanging values of variables (example), 3, 36
exponentiation program (example), 35, 53f
expressions, 22ff, 157f

factorial program (example), 35
failure (in QA4), 12, 38, 67
FIND program (example), 1, 28ff, 35, 84ff
floating-point numbers, 20ff

general solutions, 149, 166ff
generalization
    of invariants, 100
    of specifications, 147f, 161, 169ff, 173, 176
General Problem Solver, 176
generation of invariants. *See* invariants.
goal mechanism (in QA4), 11ff, 36f, 38, 66f

hypothetical reasoning, 43, 145, 151, 162, 176

identity, 50, 52
incorrectness (of programs), 37, 93ff, 119ff, 138, 140
induction (mathematical), 27, 100, 147
inequalities. *See* ordering relations.
instantiation function, 23, 63ff, 158f
interaction, 18, 41, 67, 179
INTERLISP (programming language), 2, 36

invariants
    candidate, 96
    generation of, 37, 94, 101ff, 109ff, 139, 179
    minimal, 120
    table of, 128ff
    tree, 129ff

Leibnitz's law, 40f
linear equation (example), 149
linear inequalities (example), 36
linear strategy (for simultaneous-goal problem), 155
LISP (programming language), 1, 2, 15, 22ff, 36, 143
list processing, 22ff
logical analysis (of programs), 93ff, 179
loop programs, 5ff, 22ff

matching. *See* pattern matching.
maximum of array (example), 6, 18f, 35, 69ff
minus function, 14, 37, 42, 47ff
modification (of programs), 142, 155ff, 171ff, 177 (*See also* debugging.)
monotonicity, 48
most-general match, 161, 170
most-general unifier, 173
multisets. *See* bags.
multiplication function. *See* times function.
multiplication program, integer (example), 35

nontermination of programs, 94, 120ff. *See also* termination.

optimization (of programs), 94, 175, 177, 179
ordering relations, 8, 15f, 19, 22, 28ff, 35, 37, 39ff, 47ff, 61
or function, 16, 39

partial correctness (of programs), 93, 119f
PASCAL (programming language), 1
passing backward. *See* pushing backward.
path (in program), 6ff
pattern and (in QA4), 50
pattern-directed function invocation 12ff, 143
pattern matcher (example), 22ff, 35, 63ff, 78ff, 142, 149, 157ff, 172f, 176f
pattern matching (in QA4), 11ff
percentiles (example), 28ff
permutation property (of sort program), 18
PLANNER (programming language), 142, 176
plus function, 14, 15, 37, 42, 47ff
procedural representation (of languages), 141
product function. *See* times function.
program verifier. *See* verification systems.
property lists, 15f, 40, 45
protection (in program modification), 155ff
pushing backward
    in generating verification conditions, 9
    invariant generation rule, 110f, 139
    in synthesis, 152ff
pushing forward (invariant generation rule), 111

QA4 (programming language), 2, 3, 11ff, 22, 36, 176
QLISP (programming language), 36, 142f, 176
quotient program, integer (example), 35
quotient program, real number (example), 20ff, 35

recurrence equations, 102ff, 139

recursion, formation of, 142, 146ff, 165, 176f, 180
recursive programs, verification of, 22ff
reflexivity, 18
representation of concepts, 15ff
resolution theorem proving 1, 176
reversing a list (example), 148
running time (of programs), 126f, 130, 179

sets, 143ff
    in QA4, 15f, 18, 45
side-effects, 142, 150ff, 177
simplification, 1, 13f, 27, 37, 41ff, 49ff
simultaneous goals, 142, 153ff, 176, 180. (*See also* conjunctive goals.)
sort programs (example), 18, 28ff, 36, 56ff
    exchange, 36
    three-variable, 154ff
    two-variable, 151ff, 176
specification language, 18ff, 142ff
square-root, integer (example), 150
straight-line programs, 3ff
strengthening. *See* generalization.
strip operator, 19
structural representation of knowledge, 141
structured programming, 95
substitutions, 22ff, 63ff, 78ff, 157ff, 171ff
subtract function. *See* minus function.
symmetry, 16
synthesis (of programs), 37, 140, 141ff, 179f

termination (of programs), 7, 93f, 119ff, 124ff, 146, 175, 179
tests, in generating verification conditions, 9. (*See also* conditional expressions.)
times function, 12f, 15, 37, 47f, 52f
total correctness (of programs), 119ff

transitive law, 8, 40. (*See also* ordering
    relations.)
tuples (in QA4), 15, 45

unification algorithm (example), 22,
    27ff, 35, 63ff, 142, 157, 165,
    171ff
union of two sets (example), 143ff,
    176

verification conditions, 4, 96f
    generation of, 5ff
verification systems, 1, 93, 179

weak interpretation (of programs), 139
well-founded set method (for proving
    termination), 124, 146